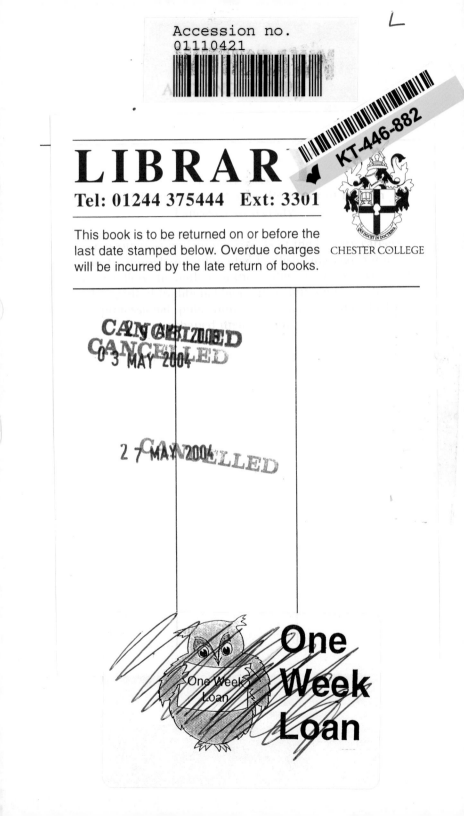

Bust of Alexander Pope by Roubiliac. (The Barber Institute of Fine Arts, University of Birmingham)

Alexander Pope

A Literary Life

Felicity Rosslyn

Lecturer in English
University of Leicester

palgrave
macmillan

First published 1990

Published by
THE MACMILLAN PRESS LTD
Houndmills, Basingstoke, Hampshire RG21 2XS
and London
Companies and representatives
throughout the world

British Library Cataloguing in Publication Data
Rosslyn, Felicity
Alexander Pope: a literary life. – (Macmillan literary
lives).
1. Poetry in English. Pope, Alexander – Biographies
I. Title
821'.5

ISBN 0–333–42690–8 (hardcover)
ISBN 0–333–42691–6 (paperback)

Transferred to digital printing, 2003

Printed and bound in Great Britain by
Antony Rowe Ltd, Chippenham and Eastbourne

For my grandfathers, H.M., H.A.M.

Contents

Preface

Some apology may be thought necessary for yet another book on Alexander Pope. He has been handsomely compensated in this century for his neglect in the last; the long-felt want of a modern biography has now been supplied by Maynard Mack, and academic industry has scrutinised his imagery, allusions, word clusters and social context until Pope himself (an indefatigable annotator) might be willing to cry 'hold, enough'.

And yet there has been no study of Pope's life and works from something approaching his own point of view, placing the stress where he might have placed it and interpreting his conduct by his own lights. It is this study I have attempted to write – at the risk, I realise, of entering so far into his point of view that I have failed to strain at gnats, and swallowed camels. My excuse is that there are numerous other studies available whose authors know better than Pope – much better – and the reader who wants to view him through modern spectacles can easily do so. I have set myself a different task, of removing the layers of old varnish from his portrait till the poet should appear as fresh and intelligible as he did to his contemporaries.

This does not mean that I have ignored the modern point of view completely. On the contrary, I have borne in mind the real difficulty of Pope's verse and his assumptions for the new reader, and much of my text has been directed to the quietly mystified student in the corner, of whom I have long experience as a teacher. But it does mean that where Pope has one explanation for an issue, and his modern commentators another, I have preferred his – and tried to elaborate it in his own voice.

The Pope of my portrait is less tormented, self-deluding and vain than usual. Whether it is a portrait to rank among the varied ones already available, the reader will judge. But it has in its favour the assumption that to be a great poet is to live by a different code of values and realities, and enables the poet to do different things with his feelings from the rest of us. He may feel as we do, but his feelings have a different issue: in art. My reason for holding to this conviction is, I admit, pure intimidation. In the course of writing about Pope he has become increasingly visible to me, as a sardonic portrait head (like the brilliant one of Roubiliac) whose muscles play across his cheeks, as he overlooks my work, with amused intelligence. When I have attempted to impose my taste or judgement upon his, he has shot me an ironic glance and murmured, 'Launch not beyond your Depth, but be discreet...'. I have submitted as gracefully as I could.

I can better understand the values of continuity and civilisation Pope wished to protect for the kindness and encouragement I have received from other Pope scholars. Dr H.H. Erskine-Hill, Professor Pat Rogers, and Maynard Mack have gallantly helped me into print at various times, and I am much indebted to their scholarship – particularly that of Maynard Mack's biography (*Alexander Pope: A Life*, 1985). In my conception of Pope and the 'literary life' I am conscious of the penetrating influence of H.A. Mason, who first showed me how literature might lead out of the study and back to life. His work on Pope has made mine a pleasure, and is the ultimate reason for the existence of this book. I hope he will not reject the burden I am laying at his door: it is, to borrow the plea of the girl with an unlooked-for baby, only a very little one.

Chronological Table

[* Approximate date]

1688 (21 May) Alexander Pope born in Lombard Street, London. The 'Glorious Revolution' sent James II into exile, and placed William of Orange on the throne.

1696* At school in a Catholic seminary in Twyford, Hants.

1697* Removed to a Catholic school in Marylebone.

1700* Pope's family moved to Binfield, Windsor Forest; he took his own education in hand, reading, imitating and translating. Martha Blount a near neighbour. Death of John Dryden.

1702 Accession of Queen Anne.

1705* Pope introduced into the literary society of London and 'adopted' by Wycherley, Garth and Walsh.

1709 *Pastorals* published. Birth of Samuel Johnson.

1711 *An Essay on Criticism* published, and acclaimed in the *Spectator*. Pope's friends included Addison, Steele, Caryll, and the Blount family.

1712 The *Messiah* published in the *Spectator*. The first (two canto) version of the *Rape of the Lock* published in a *Miscellany*, and praised by Addison. Pope's growing acquaintance with Swift, Arbuthnot, Parnell and Gay, who formed the Scriblerus Club. *Friendship with Lord Bolingbroke.

1713 *Windsor Forest* published, and proposals issued for a translation of the *Iliad*.

1714 Revised version of the *Rape of the Lock*. Death of Queen Anne and accession of George I. Whigs in power; Swift sent to Ireland, and end of the Scriblerus Club.

1715 The *Temple of Fame*. Vol. I of the *Iliad* published, causing rupture with Addison. Pope made acquaintance of Lady Mary Wortley Montagu. Jacobite rebellion.

1716 *Iliad*, Vol. II. Pope's family sold Binfield, and moved to Chiswick, near his friend and protector Lord Burlington.

1717 *Iliad*, Vol. III. Pope's first collection of *Works* published (incl. 'Eloisa to Abelard' and the 'Elegy to the Memory of an Unfortunate Lady'). Death of his father.

1718 *Iliad*, Vol. IV.

1719   Pope and his mother settled in a villa on the Thames at Twickenham.

1720   _Iliad_, Vols V and VI.

1721   Pope's edition of Parnell's _Poems_ (d. 1718).

1723   Pope's edition of the _Works_ of John Sheffield, Duke of Buckinghamshire.

1725   Pope's edition of Shakespeare, in six volumes. _Odyssey_, Vols I–III (with Broome and Fenton). Bolingbroke returned from exile (1715). *Cooling of friendship with Lady Mary Wortley Montagu.

1726   Lewis Theobald attacked Pope's Shakespeare in _Shakespeare Restored_. _Odyssey_, Vols IV–V. Swift a frequent visitor from London (_Gulliver's Travels_ (publ. October); Pope made a friend of Joseph Spence.

1727   Pope–Swift _Miscellanies_, Vols I and II. Death of George I and accession of George II.

1728   Pope–Swift _Miscellanies_, III, including provocative _Peri Bathous_. The first _Dunciad_ (in three books, with Theobald as hero) caused sensation.

1729   The _Dunciad Variorum_.

1730   Cibber appointed poet laureate.

1731   _Epistle to Burlington_ (_Moral Essay_ IV).

1732   Pope–Swift _Miscellanies_, IV (so-called 'third' volume). Death of Gay.

1733   _Epistle to Bathurst_ (_Moral Essay_ III). The first _Imitation of Horace_ (_Sat. II. i_). An _Essay on Man_, Epistles I–III. Death of Pope's mother.

1734   _Epistle to Cobham_ (_Moral Essay_ I). _Essay on Man_, Epistle IV. _Imitation of Horace_ (_Sat. II. ii_), _Sober Advice from Horace_.

1735   _Epistle to Dr Arbuthnot. Epistle to a Lady_ (_Moral Essay II_). The _Works_, Vol. II. Curll's edition of Pope's letters. Death of Arbuthnot.

1737   _Imitations of Horace_ (_Eps II. i, II. ii_). Pope's authorised edition of his letters. Attack on the _Essay on Man_ by Crousaz.

1738   _Imitations of Horace_ (_Eps I. vi, I. i_). _Epilogue to the Satires_. _Essay on Man_ defended by Warburton.

1740   Pope made a friend of Warburton. Cibber's _Apology for his Life_.

1741   Pope embarked with Warburton on the definitive edition of his works.

1742   The _New Dunciad_ (i.e. Book IV). Resignation of Walpole.

1743   The *Dunciad* in four books, with Cibber replacing Theobald.
        Pope's health declined.
1744   Death of Pope (30 May).

Introduction

A 'literary life' of Pope might almost be thought a tautology – for Pope had little life that was not literary, and few lives have been so completely fulfilled in terms of literature. It is not often given to a poet both to know what he can do, and then to do it. Pope was one of the few; and in a small way, that has been his misfortune, for there is something very irritating to the human spirit in such a spectacle. The Romantic poets, said Byron, ostracised Pope for the same reason the Athenians gave for their ostracism of Aristides – they were 'tired of hearing him always called "The Just"'. Pope has been disliked for his comprehensiveness, his formal perfection and simply for seeming to embody the eighteenth century. In a minor key, many students have a version of the Romantic response, when they recognise the polish of the style and suspect how many decisions have gone into its brilliance – but resent it nonetheless, for it seems to have no need of them: it leaves them without anything to add.

The value of a 'literary life' is that it can suggest where the polish came from, and humanise what seems inhumanly perfect in Pope's achievement. If, as Byron said, he is the only poet whose perfection has been made his reproach, the best way to remove the stigma is to show what that perfection of style was for, and to recreate for the reader the depths that underlie the striking surface. We may take our cue from G. Wilson Knight, who has insisted on the humanity of Pope's seemingly artificial art. Pope's words, he says, 'are not snatched cold from the outer void of mental speculation or divine aspiration; they are warm, like a rich necklace warm from human contact . . . they are valuable with the value we attach to an heirloom, or some old volume once in famous hands.'[1] Nothing could better convey the meaning of Pope's allusiveness, which to the uninitiated reader merely serves to widen the gulf between Pope's world and his: Pope's words are heirlooms, and much of their significance comes from their past history in other hands. Pope is a learned writer, not for scholarship's sake, but from a sense of responsibility: he must know where each word came from, and what work it has done in the past, before he can decide what work it can do in the present. But this is only the beginning of communication. What follows is his gift to us, his readers, of that

1

accumulated wealth – the placing in our hands of those historic volumes, or the clasping round our necks of those warm pearls. The single great aim of Pope's poetry is that bequest; and it is in the hope of increasing the number of readers who can view themselves as Pope's legatees (rather than inevitably dispossessed by the passage of time, or a non-classical education) that this book has been written.

A literary life of Pope may also hope to explain some of the paradoxes of his behaviour that still darken his public reputation, for all recent scholarship has done to improve it. The problem here, I suspect, is a misunderstanding about the kind of 'humanity' we should attribute to a great poet. It is a common conviction that a poet is as 'human' as the rest of us, only more so – more inclined to wine, women and song, or (in the case of a satirist like Pope) more angry or vain. When Pope's Victorian editor Elwin discovered that Pope had tampered with some of the correspondence he printed, he leapt to the conclusion that Pope was 'human' in a most derogatory sense, a view still prevailing in some quarters;[2] and when we add to this Pope's physical deformity, we have a context in which it is easy to patronise Pope as a thwarted human being, all-too-humanly using his poetical gift for private ends, and suffering as any human being would suffer in his predicament.

The problem here, perhaps, is with the word 'humanity.' It begins to be synonymous with 'weakly human, flawed' and to be a way of bringing the poet within our reach by insisting on the similarity of his clay. I would make a different assumption: that in some ways a poet is highly unlike the rest of us, not 'human' at all – and that when he has humanity, it is in a very selective sense. We know Chekhov's opinion of what the literary life does to one's humanity, expressed by a writer in *The Seagull*:

> It's such a barbarous life. Here am I talking to you and getting quite excited, yet can't forget for a second that I've an unfinished novel waiting for me. Or I see a cloud over there like a grand piano. So I think it must go in a story. 'A cloud like a grand piano sailed past. ' . . . I try to catch every sentence, every word you and I say and quickly lock all these sentences and words away in my literary storehouse because they might come in handy. . . . I feel I'm taking pollen from my best flowers, tearing them up and stamping on the roots – all to make honey that goes to some vague, distant destination. I'm mad, I must be.[3]

The artist then seduces and abandons the girl to whom he makes this confession, and she comes to see what she has been to him: 'a plot for a short story'.

Thus, the assumption I would start from is rather paradoxical in view of how often I shall be talking about Pope's moral values: that the great artist is utterly amoral and no matter what he pretends to be doing (as Trigorin here is pretending to confess), what he is really doing is working at his art. He may be ashamed of living among his friends as a fifth-columnist, and cultivate a careful appearance of normality, but we should not be deceived. His mind has the dreadful pertinacity of the bee in pursuit of nectar: he is thinking about honey, and the flowers are merely nectar-depots to him.

It follows from this that a literary life is not like the biography of a normal person. It has less to do with what actually happened to the poet than with what he made out of what happened. He lives in the most radical sense only from poem to poem: 'For a poet poems are real experiences', a reviewer of Mack's biography has recently insisted, and 'as a man may be changed by a love affair or a bereavement, so a poet may be changed by a work of imagination – somebody else's or his own'.[4] It is in this spirit I have taken the poems themselves as the key to Pope's literary life in what follows, and preferred them as evidence, not only to what his contemporaries thought he was doing, but to what he himself may have claimed (since no one ever pretended more assiduously to be 'normal', or disguised his nectar-collecting more deviously). This is the sense in which I think we must say that an artist has less humanity than other people: he is, like Trigorin, a dangerous person to be near. But the sense in which we must grant him true humanity is in being able to turn nectar into honey, and then to share it with us. We, after all, are the 'vague, distant destination' of his efforts; but for his sense of our needs, his nurturing instincts could leave him in peace.

It follows from this view of the artist's priorities that he does not so much write to live, as live in order to write. This is another paradoxical proposition, given how successfully Pope carved a fortune for himself from his powers and created the reading public to support him. Undoubtedly, he wrote to live; but it is at least as true that he lived his life to make poetry from it – and that the form it took was the form his poetry gave it. We can see this at work in his notorious relations with the 'Dunces', for instance, which have often been interpreted as part of his human frailty: a fight in the mud in which Pope himself was plentifully bespattered, and did damage to his reputation which has dogged him to our own time. But it would be truer to see his quarrel with the Dunces as the by-product of any literary life. For the artist whose mind is wholly and obsessively devoted to his next work, who is as much 'possessed' by his art as the bee is by genetic programming, the sight of another who also considers himself to be an artist, but has no notion that he must reach his goal by selflessness and labour, is passionately provoking. It is at once funny and dreadfully unnatural – as if a drone should learn to buzz and blunder in and out of flowers, and feel proud of himself for his dusting of yellow, though quite unequipped to gather nectar and put it to use. The artist and the Dunce are natural enemies. Pope takes for granted 'the constant and eternal aversion of all bad writers to a good one'[5] and shows a calm contempt for them on all occasions. We can understand the animus the Dunces must have felt when we hear him remarking coolly to Spence, the collector of his conversation,

> Middling poets are no poets at all. There is always a great number of such in each age that are almost totally forgotten in the next. A few curious inquirers may know that there were such men and that they wrote such and such things, but to the world they are as if they had never been.[6]

We should remember this detachment when we are tempted to think of Pope's battle with the Dunces as springing from wounded vanity – or to see his aggression as unprovoked. The Dunce offers the provocation by mistaking his own gifts, and he gets his reward by being 'totally forgotten'. If Pope also laughs at him in a Dunciad, that is because in the truly literary life, no experience is ever wasted.

The artist, I am assuming, is always converting his experience into honey, and even painful, comic or repulsive experience is nectar to him. This makes the experience of being alive radically different for the artist and the Dunce. The artist may, at the human level, show rather less conscience: it is 'barbarous', as Trigorin says, to be collecting cloud-impressions while your interlocutor is falling in love with you; but that is because he needs all the conscience he has for the task of creation, without which nothing of the experience of being alive will remain. He is aware of the gulf of oblivion waiting for all of us. He is also aware that half-measures are not enough: to the world it is as if the quite-good poets and their quite-good poetry 'had never been'. Verse that would endure wind and weather must be more tightly constructed; the transformation of life into art must be so complete that the art can stand by itself.

I take it this is the explanation for much that seems oblique or reprehensible in Pope's behaviour towards his contemporaries. As a man, he often had a bad conscience about it (as, for instance, in his embarrassed equivocations over the publishing of his correspondence), but he never let this bad conscience prevail: his conscience as an artist was what most deeply concerned him, and this was perfectly clear. He was taking responsibility for what he alone could do – not from arrogance, but from a tormenting perception of the alternative:

> Vain was the chief's and sage's pride
> They had no Poet and they dyd!
> In vain they schem'd, in vain they bled
> They had no Poet and are dead![7]

This may also be the explanation for his general pleasure in artifice. As Johnson remarks in his *Life* of Pope, with dignified wonder,

In all his intercourse with mankind he had great delight in artifice, and endeavoured to attain all his purposes by indirect and unsuspected methods. 'He hardly drank tea without a strategem.'[8]

This sounds like a version of the artist's perennial interest in appearance and truth. How can life be nudged into the desired shape, without his apparent interference? How is the appearance of reality created, and how does the mind apprehend it? Living, as the artist does, between two worlds, the one already created, and the other requiring to be born, he has a much more elastic sense of 'reality' than the rest of us, and understands that – quite contrary to the usual assumption – 'truth' is an honorific term we bestow on something that convinces us. It is not an ethical judgement at all, but a technical one; and his great aim in life is to understand how that triumph was achieved. What is it that turns a private letter into a publishable one? What is it that converts a familiar friend into a

public icon? How does human language – perishable, lively
spontaneous – become imperishable poetic utterance?

Just as Trigorin's mind is constantly taking notes, and making
technical observations, I take it a glimpse inside Pope's would have
revealed something quite foreign to the rest of us: a starkly
professional interest in what was going on around him. 'What
could I do with this character, or theme, or grouping, or emotion?'
we may imagine him thinking; while some way towards the back
of his mind we should we have heard the rhythmic pulse of new
lines emerging into being, and the whisper of words looking for a
rhyme. It would be futile to appeal to such an onlooker that our
own sense of ourselves was radiantly unique. He is interested in
his art, and only so much of our nature as can be assimilated to its
meaning; he is not even attempting to see us innocently, for what
we are. As Ernst Gombrich has demonstrated in terms of the visual
arts, there is no such thing as the 'innocent eye', guilelessly
examining reality for its true nature. The artist thinks in patterns
first, and only secondarily in terms of what is really visible around
him. Every observation presupposes a question, and every question a prior assumption; Pope's eye, searching among his acquaintance for instances of wit, candour, frigidity or corruption, invariably found what it was looking for – and obliterated whatever was
incommensurate with the overall effect with perfect *sang-froid*. In
art there are no questions about justice and charity, only about
what is fitting, and not fitting.

It follows from the peculiar priorities of the literary life that its
pleasures, too, are peculiar. Pope may seem to have been barred
from the obvious pleasures of life by illness, but nothing debarred
him from the primary pleasure of the artist, his joy in creation.
This, after all, is what the artist is born to do, and everything that
ministers to that end is pleasurable to him. We would be naive, for
instance, to suppose that satire records disgust and disapproval in
any simple form; disgust and disapproval supply the occasion, but
hatred is not sufficiently creative to produce true satire. Love must
intermingle with the satirist's emotions before he can fully recreate
what it is he satirises, and embody it vigorously enough for us to
see it too. It takes joy and affection to satirise successfully: under
his breath the artist is praying, 'Please, do it again! Just once!' He
would not have the object of his aversion any less wonderfully
repulsive than it is; it is precisely the repulsiveness that he
cherishes, because that is what makes his poem possible. On this

assumption, there is no reason to suppose that Pope was an unhappy man, or even an angry one at the core: the impersonality which every true artist possesses means that, like God, he is constantly looking at his creation, and seeing that it is good – or, if that analogy seems too Romantic, that he can always say, with the mother goose to her daughter, 'My dear, you are a perfect goose!'

If the artist's pleasures are different from ours, and his standards of truth and falsehood, we should not be surprised to find what offends him is different too. We noted above that for the true artist, the sight of a Dunce who has mistaken his calling is passionately provoking. Yet it might seem that he has only to avert his gaze; the Dunce hurts no one but himself, and is more to be pitied than blamed. Why is it impossible for the artist to leave the quarrel here? A lapse of artistic taste, which affects ordinary mortals as nothing more than a lapse, affects him, it seems, as a menace as terrible as the famous hole in the Dutch dyke: a threat to the whole laborious construct of art, which only the artist who has borne the labour of constructing it knows in all its vulnerability. Those of us who take our responsibilities more lightly suppose that such constructs are as solid as they appear; he knows that just as it was constructed by human effort, so human laxity can undo it. He also knows that it is not the dyke alone that is threatened, but ourselves – for what we take to be our 'self' is, like the dyke, a construct, generated in the effort to build those things outside ourselves, like law, philosophy, and above all, art, which in return help us to be what we are. The bee builds an astonishingly elaborate structure outside himself, in the form of a hive, which helps him solve the problems of his existence; and man, through language, constructs more miraculously still.[9] If art is the place where we become our 'selves', then the bad artist is not merely a bad workman, but the profoundest of traitors. He can make us less than we might have been, or he can undo what we were. Nothing he does is irrelevant to us, for he works in our shared medium of existence, language.

Bad art, in this sense, is a kind of crime, akin to poisoning the public wells. This is why the true artist cannot tolerate it, and why his struggle against it is unremitting. 'The life of a Wit' – that is, someone aware of these distinctions – 'is a warfare upon earth', Pope remarked early in his career, and the rest of his life was a long demonstration of it.[10] When we consider what Pope was protecting, and with what skill he located and reinforced the weak places in the dyke of our common culture, we may better understand why

Byron viewed him as a hero of civilisation, whose works made up a more comprehensive record of what mankind had built than anyone else's – not excluding Shakespeare's:

If any great national or natural convulsion could or should overwhelm your country in such sort as to sweep Great Britain from the kingdoms of the earth, and leave only that, after all, the most living of dead things, a *dead language*, to be studied and read, and imitated, by the wise of future and far generations, upon foreign shores; if your literature should become the learning of mankind, divested of party cabals, temporary fashions, and national pride and prejudice; – an Englishman, anxious that the posterity of strangers should know that there had been such a thing as a British Epic and Tragedy, might wish for the preservation of Shakespeare and Milton; but the surviving World would snatch Pope from the wreck, and let the rest sink with the people. He is the moral poet of all civilisation; and as such, let us hope that he will one day be the national poet of mankind.[11]

It was in the hope that this might some day be said of him that Pope lived and wrote. We are not likely to misunderstand him if we bear this in mind, and do not attempt to interpret him by the lights of a commoner form of humanity.

Nonetheless he was as much of a human being as the rest of us, and would have had no experience to add to the common store if he had not been condemned to live and die in the flesh like everyone else. We are bound to be curious about the way he led his existence, and to ask biographical questions which (in Johnson's noble conception of the value of biography) help elicit 'what comes near to ourselves, what we can turn to use'.[12] In stressing that Pope was also an artist, I am merely redressing an imbalance that naturally occurs when readers interpret his life as something other than a literary one. To return to my starting point, the first and best explanation of Pope's behaviour, at its strangest and most paradoxical, is usually that his mind was on his art; and where most readers coming to Pope for the first time are struck by the fact that he was a cripple, and ambitious, and a genius (in that order), I would put it the other way around – that Pope was a genius, who was therefore ambitious, and who happened to be a cripple. The paradoxes there are in the nature of his humanity and his ethics, arise under pressure from forces (I would suggest) that few human beings have experienced in the same degree.

The first of these forces is implicit in everything that has been said so far: that is, the force of creative genius, which made the ordinary assumption that reality is one thing, and art another, seem a dreadful truncation of possibilities. Pope was constantly exploring the ways in which art made reality more real, and life made art more artistic. His work lay in that crepuscular area where Aristotle said a 'credible untruth' was preferable to an 'incredible truth', and his conscience as an artist was quite immovable on this matter (though not quite his conscience as a man, as we shall see).

The second of these forces was Pope's extraordinary intelligence, which committed him to a life of irritability and disingenuousness, if only because he habitually saw what others did not, or saw it before they did – which is not polite in any society. From the moment he awoke to consciousness as the son of a linen-merchant, surrounded by those for whom language, faith and meaning were all equally straightforward matters, it was clear to Pope that perceptions like his, required also the knowledge of how to render those perceptions visible to others; and that intelligence which could not render its knowledge lovable undercut its own purposes. Unlike many geniuses, Pope exerted himself to make friends with people as intelligent as himself, and those he could admire to the point of adulation for qualities he did not possess, by way of disciplining the arrogance that a great gift brings with it; and if we sometimes sense behind the vaulting ambition of the poetry a power of destructiveness barely reined in, perhaps we should be surprised that he did no more harm than he did, and that, knowing how little anyone else could restrain him, he found so many ways of restraining himself.

The third force under which he operated was clearly his physical deformity, following on from tuberculosis of the spine, which left him with a short, spindly, hunchbacked form, and a lifetime of chills and headaches. Probably the full effect of deformity is something we could not hope to gauge in another person, and would find it hard enough to assess in ourselves. Pope kept his own counsel on the subject, and only expressed as much pain and sensitivity about it to his friends as their feelings would bear. What we may deduce with some certainty is that the strain of being trapped in the outer form of Homer's twisted Thersites, while as conscious of his destiny and high gifts as another Achilles, set

Pope the supreme conundrum of his existence. How can art mend the shortcomings of reality? How can the imagination create more potent realities than the eye apprehends, and how lastingly? What is 'truth'? He permitted few full-length portraits of himself, and chose rather to be represented in busts which threw into relief his Roman head, bright eye, and long, clever nose. In this dignified guise, his form could be found 'in twenty noblemen's houses', as Voltaire noted with astonishment on his visit to England (no man of letters had comparable status in France). Pope taught his contemporaries how to see the immortal part of himself in the mortal; and it is a tribute to how thoroughly he identified with it himself, that we read his verse with no sense that what we are reading is the work of a man radically disabled by nature from leading the life of the rest of his kind. If we had been able to meet him in the flesh, our pity might have dropped away from us as quickly as Voltaire's. Voltaire, says Goldsmith,

> has often told his friends that he never observed in himself such a succession of opposite passions as he experienced upon his first interview with Mr. Pope. When he first entered the room, and perceived our poor melancholy English poet naturally deformed, and wasted as he was with sickness and study, he could not help regarding him with the utmost compassion. But, when Mr. Pope began to speak, and to reason upon moral obligations, and dress the most delicate sentiments in the most charming diction, Voltaire's pity began to be changed into admiration and at last even into envy.[13]

The interplay of the harshest factual limitation and a boundingly creative imaginative power – which subdues posterity, as it was intended to – marks Pope's literary life from end to end.

1

Early Life and Juvenilia

EDUCATION AND EARLY CAREER

Alexander Pope was born on 21 May 1688 in London, to an elderly linen-merchant and his second wife. He was their only son, though there was a daughter from the first marriage, and he was correspondingly treasured through a happy early childhood, in which he rapidly discovered that his business was with words – while his proud but sober father impressed on him that there was room for improvement in this, as in all else. Joseph Spence records Pope's mother saying in later life,

> Mr Pope's father . . . was no poet, but he used to set him to make English verses when very young. He was pretty difficult in being pleased and used often to send him back to new turn them. 'These are not good rhymes' he would say, for that was my husband's word for verses.[1]

The young Pope's education probably owes more to this, and his own excited explorations in the family library, than anything else. He also told Spence,

> I had learned very early to read and delighted extremely in it. I taught myself to write very early, too, by copying from printed books with which I used to divert myself, as other children do with scrawling out pictures.[2]

The poet-to-be developed the intensity of relationship with books that other children develop with their favourite toys, and a fascination with books as artefacts that lasted all his life.

Pope's more formal education was radically affected by the fact that his parents were Roman Catholics. To be Catholic at this time was to be treated as an alien in one's own country, to be suspected of Jacobitism and to come under automatic legal penalties. In particular, no Catholic could attend a public school or university; and such Catholic schools as were tolerated, were mostly confined to quiet corners of the country. The young Pope was therefore taught the rudiments of grammar and the Greek alphabet by a priest at home, and then at various little schools, beginning with one at Twyford, near Winchester. The schools left scant impression on him, and his residences were brief: perhaps the atmosphere of pietism was more than he could bear (Pope never became a Catholic in a fervent enough sense for his co-religionists, though typically enough, he never became Anglican enough for his Anglican friends either) or perhaps the beatings that were considered an indispensable aid to learning had just the opposite effect on him. At any rate, by the time he was twelve, he seems to have felt that his education lay in his own power, which was just where he wanted it; and after his father moved to Binfield in Berkshire, presumably in deference to the 'ten-mile rule' which forbade Catholics to live nearer London, he took French and Italian lessons and worked fervently at his studies by himself. He represents this to Spence as the happiest mode of education he could have fallen into:

When I had done with my priests I took to reading by myself, for which I had a very great eagerness and enthusiasm, especially for poetry.... In a few years I had dipped into a great number of the English, French, Italian, Latin, and Greek poets. This I did without any design but that of pleasing myself, and got the languages by hunting after the stories in the several poets I read, rather than read the books to get the languages. I followed everywhere as my fancy led me, and was like a boy gathering flowers in the woods and fields just as they fall in his way. I still look upon these five or six years as the happiest part of my life.[3]

The Popes had some distinguished neighbours in Binfield, including a retired secretary of state, Sir William Trumbull, and that part of his education Pope did not get by devouring books in this way, he got by keeping company with affectionate elders like Sir William, who were delighted by his precocity and proud to encourage his early productions. In the course of his teens Pope was introduced to a widening circle of 'the great' in London – the literary great of the last age, as well as the aristocracy. He got to know the poet and critic William Walsh, who was an old associate of John Dryden (1631–1700), the English poet from whose work Pope learned most, and Samuel Garth (1661–1719), another of Dryden's friends, a physician and author of a medical mock-epic. He became the friend and even ghost-writer of William Wycherley (1640–1716), who in his old age was glad to have his rambling verses polished by a younger hand; and when Pope finally appeared in print, with a set of four *Pastorals* (1709), he could proudly consider himself to have received the plaudits of the great world in advance:

> These Pastorals were written at the age of sixteen, and then past thro' the hands of Mr. *Walsh*, Mr. *Wycherley*, G. *Granville*, afterwards Lord *Lansdown*, Sir *William Trumbal*, Dr. *Garth*, Lord *Halifax*, Lord *Somers*, Mr. *Mainwaring*, and others. All these gave our Author the greatest encouragement, and particularly Mr. *Walsh*, (whom Mr. *Dryden*, in his Postscript to Virgil, calls the best critic of his age.)[4]

Clearly, the self-educated son of an obscure tradesman found no difficulty in launching his career. His various patrons might have their individual reasons for taking notice of this rising star – as Wycherley made use of Pope's pen, Lord Halifax hoped for the 'puffery' of his adopted authors and Mainwaring had Whig patronage to dispense – but their unanimous motive is unmistakably a respect for Pope's powers. He enters their world as a master – and there he remains.

JUVENILIA, 1700–1709

It may seem that Pope's education was sadly wanting, and does nothing to explain this meteoric rise and rapid acceptance on the part of literary London. Later in his career, Pope's enemies made great capital of the fact that he was not a 'university man', and when he had the temerity to translate the whole of Homer, voices were heard complaining on every side that he did not possess enough Greek to do it. Yet Pope was increasingly certain as he got older that he was, as he told Spence,

> better in some respects for not having had a regular education. He (as he observed in particular) read originally for the sense,

whereas we are taught for so many years to read only for words.[5]

By reading for pleasure he kept intact that subtle web of connection between the meaning of words, and the rapturous increase of power that accompanies their discovery, which a regular schooling so easily ruptures. He also worked at foreign languages as a means to an end – not as an end in themselves, as they rapidly become in school. He learnt languages because he wanted stories; he bothered with words, because he craved sense:

> I did not follow the grammar, but rather hunted in the authors for a syntax of my own, and then began translating any parts that pleased me particularly in the best Greek and Latin poets. By that means I formed my taste, which I think verily at about sixteen was very near as good as it is now.[6]

Though a teacher of languages might wince at the casual attitude implied to accuracy, we see how Pope never imbibed the deadly notion that the dictionary and grammar embody the truth of a language. He learnt what words and phrases must mean, because of their context, and made his translations, not to please a master, but for a much better reason: to bring treasures across from another language into his own. He stumbled, in fact, on to the archetypal method of humanist education; and it may seem less strange to our modern eyes if we look on him as the last in a line of Renaissance poets who gave their childhoods to the poetry of the past – just like Dante in thirteenth-century Florence, as Boccaccio tells us:

> With laudable desire for perpetual fame, scorning those riches that are but for a season, he freely gave himself to the desire of having full knowledge of the fictions of the poets, and the exposition thereof by the rules of art. In which exercise he became the closest intimate of Virgil, of Horace, of Ovid, of Statius, and of every other famous poet, not only loving to know them, but also in lofty verse striving to imitate them; even as his works, whereof we shall discourse hereafter in their time, make manifest.[7]

Five centuries later, Pope became 'the closest intimate' of these same Roman poets, 'not only loving to know them, but . . . striving to imitate them' on his own account; and this is how he acquired the staggering maturity of style and content which brought him such instantaneous success in London. It is also how he laid the foundations for that characteristic of his language we noted before, that for all its public gloss, it breathes intimacy with the author's life, 'like a rich necklace warm from human contact'. The years spent in intimacy with the living dead (Pope would have echoed Byron's conviction that a 'dead language' was 'the most living of dead things') are what generated that warmth, and gave him the familiarity with the past that enables him to put his poetry within our grasp like 'some old volume once in famous hands'. Like a passionate bibliophile, he can recount the history of all his treasures: he knows how many favourite lines of Virgil are lines of Homer, how many of Statius are from Virgil, and how many of Milton and Dryden are from all three. And unlike the bibliophile, he knows that none of these treasures can be procured by any means save active recreation. 'It is easier to steal the club of Hercules', says the old maxim, 'than a line of Homer.'

It is difficult for those of us who have had a modern education to grasp the value of 'imitation' in a poet's development, or to take the force of this distinction between stealing from other poets, and recreation. The problem is compounded by the dull sound of the term 'neo-classicism', which is usually applied to this imitation of the classics. But the meaning of the prefix 'neo-' is 'new', and neo-classicism, as Pope and his friends understood it, was the living child of living parents – or it did not deserve the term. They had nothing but contempt for those who revered the works of the past for their rust, and valued them over the works of the present because they showed no disturbing signs of animation. For the true 'new classicist' the Renaissance was still going on, and old life was giving birth to new, as it always had done.

Nonetheless, we may be tempted to wonder, what became of originality under such an educational regime? What authenticity could there be in the midst of such deference, and how did the poet inside Pope survive? These are post-Romantic doubts, which stem from the Romantic emphasis on feeling as the source of poetry – the assumption made by the young W.B. Yeats, for instance:

I tried . . . to write out of my emotions exactly as they came to me in life, not changing them to make them more beautiful. 'If I can be sincere and make my language natural, and without becom-

ing discursive, like a novelist, and so indiscreet and prosaic,' I
said to myself, 'I shall, if good luck or bad luck make my life
interesting, be a great poet; for it will no longer be a matter of
literature at all.'

Alas, the hope that authenticity could be achieved by mere
abstinence was a vain one, and the mature Yeats acknowledged as
much:

> Yet when I re-read those early poems which gave me so much
> trouble, I find little but romantic convention, unconscious
> drama.[8]

Trusting to his feelings, Yeats only conjured up the heavy-lidded
pre-Raphaelite ghosts of the previous generation, and made them
speak in the language of a dead convention.

Pope would not have been at all surprised; for he knew that
poems were not made out of feelings, necessary as these were for
the initial inspiration. Poems were made out of words, and words
would always tend to do what they had done before. The poet
could never reach the point where 'it would no longer be a matter
of literature at all', because literature would always resemble other
literature more than it resembled anything else. And if it did not, so
much the worse, for it would be unintelligible: like a language
spoken by only one person, there would be no way of deciphering
it. The way out of the trap of inauthenticity, he would have said, is
not to evade this literariness, but to put it to work; not to lose
oneself in the past, but to find oneself there. This is an enterprise
no less demanding of authenticity: for adjudicating between what
the past brings, and what one can properly accept of that wealth, is
as delicate a business as accepting presents from loving, but
over-generous parents. At the same time, it acknowledges the
biological fact there is no denying; our parents gave birth to us, and
the shape of our chin needs no further explanation. As Pope says,
in laying his first poems before the public,

> They who say our thoughts are not our own because they
> resemble the Ancients, may as well say our faces are not our
> own, because they are like our Fathers.[9]

It was in this effort to 'find himself' in the past, and lay claim to however much of the inheritance might be properly his, that the young Pope spent so much of his education in imitating the Greek, Roman and English classics. Mankind through the ages had pronounced epic poetry to be the noblest effort of the imagination; therefore he would write his own epic, in four books of a thousand lines, which turned out to be a salutary lesson, however, in how *not* to relate to one's parents:

> I endeavoured (says he, smiling) in this poem to collect all the beauties of the great epic writers into one piece. There was Milton's style in one part and Cowley's in another, here the style of Spenser imitated and there of Statius, here Homer and Virgil, and there Ovid and Claudian.
>
> 'It was an imitative poem then, as your other exercises were imitations of this or that story?' asked Spence.
>
> Just that ... Alcander was a prince, driven from his throne by Deucalion, father of Minos, and some other princes. It was better planned than Blackmore's *Prince Arthur*, but as slavish an imitation of the ancients. Alcander showed all the virtue of suffering, like Ulysses, and of courage, like Aeneas or Achilles. Apollo as the patron of Rhodes was his great defender, and Cybele as the patroness of Deucalion and Crete his great enemy. She raises a storm against him in the first book as Juno does against Aeneas, and he is cast away and swims ashore just as Ulysses does to the island of Phaecia.[10]

We need not feel regret that Pope was later circumspect enough to do away with the surviving manuscript: nothing could better demonstrate the difference between, as he says, 'slavish' imitation, and the recreation of a classic in new terms. But even here we can see how intimate a knowledge he had acquired of the way epic poems actually work: of the tension they all dramatise between opposing powers that operate over the head of the hero, of the value of a shipwreck in setting the narrative going, and the nature of a hero's virtues. What is missing is a new goal for this technical expertise – he does not as yet have anything to add.

Pope also works his way through the styles and subjects of the last generation of English poets, Cowley and Waller, Dorset and Rochester. He tries to catch their accent and rhythm; sometimes he thinks he can improve on their metre or clarity. In every case he examines the wealth of the past to see whether he has the right to inherit it. In the case of Cowley the answer is in the affirmative: the cavalier poet and exile sings the praises of a life of retirement and quiet integrity in terms Pope was to reiterate ever more loudly, to the end of his career. But even at an age when his likeliest feeling about solitude was that he had enough of it and to spare, Pope can catch the tone of old experience:

Ode On Solitude[11]
Happy the Man, who free from Care,
  The Business and the Noise of Towns,
Contented breaths his Native Air,
               In his own Grounds. . . .

Blest, who can unconcern'dly find
  His Years slide silently away,
In Health of Body, Peace of Mind,
               Quiet by Day,

Repose at Night; Study and Ease,
Together mixt; sweet Recreation;
And Innocence, which most does please,
               With Meditation.

Thus, let me live, unseen, unknown,
  Thus, unlamented, let me die,
Steal from the World, and not a Stone
               Tell where I lye.

This piece of premature philosophy reveals how thoroughly Pope has absorbed his reading. The first verse grows out of Cowley's translation of Horace's most famous poem about the value of country retirement, now firmly shaped into Sapphic metre:

Happy the Man whom bounteous Gods allow
With his own Hands Paternal Grounds to plough!
Like the first golden Mortals Happy he
From Business and the cares of Money free!

The next verse elaborates Cowley's translation of Martial,

Thus let my life slide silently away
With Sleep all Night, and Quiet all the Day,

while the last verse of elegant gloom is worked up from his translation of a chorus of Seneca's, a favourite of the wounded veterans of court life in all periods:

> Here wrapt in th'Arms of Quiet let me ly, . . .
> Here let my Life, with as much silence slide . . .
> Nor let my homely Death embroidered be
>   With Scutcheon or with Elegie.
> An old Plebean let me Dy.[12]

This dates (according to Pope) from his twelfth year; at thirteen, he apprentices himself to the Metaphysicals, and writes hyperbolical verses to a nonexistent lady. Edmund Waller had excelled at conjuring poetry from minimal subjects, as may be seen from such titles as 'The Apology of *Sleep* for not approaching the Lady who can do any thing but sleep when she pleaseth' and equally, 'Of the Lady who can sleep when she pleaseth' – not to mention 'Of a Tree cut in paper' and, more desperately yet, 'To a Lady, from whom he received the foregoing Copy, which for many years had been lost'. The apprentice abandons himself to this flagrant foolery and spins out his nonsense on the subject 'Of the Lady who could not sleep in a stormy Night':

> As gods sometimes descend from heav'n and deign
> On earth a while with mortals to remain,
> So gentle sleep from *Serenissa* flies,
> To dwell at last upon her lover's eyes. . . .
>
>   (1–4)

He is borrowing Waller's figure and turning it round:

> No wonder Sleep from careful Lovers flies,
> To bathe himself in Sacharissa's Eyes.[13]

Pope also masters here the art of balancing his paradoxes, of compressing his sense into the two halves of a couplet, and turning a sequence of gentle reproaches into a final compliment – the adroitness that makes Waller's poetry not quite negligible:

> That god's indulgence can she justly crave,
> Who flies the tyrant to relieve the slave?

Or should those eyes alone that rest enjoy,
Which in all others they themselves destroy?
Let her whom fear denies repose to take,
Think for her love what crowd of wretches wake.
So us'd to sighs, so long inur'd to tears,
Are winds and tempests dreadful to her ears?
Jove with a nod may bid the world to rest,
But *Serenissa* must becalm the breast.

(5–14)

A year later, and we find the young poet playing with the art of barbed compliment, in the manner of that aristocratic wit, the Earl of Dorset. This poem subsumes much reading of Dryden, too, who had long ago satirised the same poet, Elkanah Settle, and produced an irresistible subject for imitation in his 'Succession' poem, 'Mac Flecknoe' (1682). The apprentice slips into the mode of elegant insult with ease: here is a role he will play again and again, most formidably in the *Dunciad*, reusing many of these same jokes, indeed:

To the Author of a Poem, intitled, Successio[14]
Begone ye Criticks, and restrain your Spite,
Codrus writes on, and will for ever write;
The heaviest Muse the swiftest Course has gone,
As Clocks run fastest when most Lead is on.
What tho' no Bees around your Cradle flew,
Nor on your Lips distill'd their golden Dew?
Yet have we oft discover'd in their stead,
A Swarm of Drones, that buzz'd about your Head.
When you, like *Orpheus*, strike the warbling Lyre,
Attentive Blocks stand round you, and admire.
Wit, past thro' thee, no longer is the same,
As Meat digested takes a diff'rent Name;
But Sense must sure thy safest Plunder be,
Since no Reprizals can be made on thee.
Thus thou may'st Rise, and in thy daring Flight
(Tho' ne'er so weighty) reach a wondrous height;
So, forc'd from Engines, Lead it self can fly,
And pondrous Slugs move nimbly thro' the Sky.
Sure *Bavius* copy'd *Mævius* to the full,
And *Chærilus* taught *Codrus* to be dull;

Therefore, dear Friend, at my Advice give o'er
This needless Labour, and contend no more,
To prove a dull *Succession* to be true,
Since 'tis enough we find it so in You.

The jokes are a little heavy and roundabout – the mature Pope
would never have settled for so blunt a witticism as that 'Swarm of
Drones', or so choppy a line as, 'Yet have we oft discover'd in their
stead' – but here already are his wicked handling of repetition
('*Codrus* writes on, and will for ever write'), and his scatological
politeness ('As Meat digested takes a diff'rent Name'). Still more
characteristic is his metaphysical delight in paradox, much more
vigorously exercised than in his imitation of Waller, and more like
a new mode of thought than an exercise: the idea that leaden poets
may 'rise in daring Flight' just as lead slugs 'move nimbly thro' the
Sky' enchants him. Together with the lead weights on the mechan-
ism of clocks (l.4) it was to reappear in the *Dunciad*, over twenty
years later, as a leaden writer's explanation for his genius:

> As forc'd from wind-guns, lead itself can fly,
> And pond'rous slugs cut swiftly thro' the sky;
> As clocks to weight their nimble motion owe,
> The wheels above urg'd by the load below;
> Me, Emptiness and Dulness could inspire,
> And were my Elasticity and Fire.
>
> (I, 177–82)

Equally characteristic is the thought that a dull poetical 'Succession' and a dull Monarchy support one another (it was the
Hanoverian Succession that Settle had been praising, in advance).
This is the idea at the heart of Pope's last poem, the revised *Dunciad*
(1742), where the somnolence of the Hanoverian court, and the
dullness of its poet laureate, lead to the final collapse of that Dutch
dyke of civilisation Pope saw himself as protecting. And equally
characteristic too, Wycherley might have added, is the fact that 'As
Clocks run fastest when most Lead is on' (l.4) is a line from one of
his poems that he passed over to Pope for revision; a nice example
of the way that, as a contemporary remarked, if Pope 'met with a
good line (even in a much inferior poet) he would take it (like a lord
of the manor) for his own'.[15]
But perhaps the nicest example of what the young apprentice

learnt by imitation is in his version of the famous poem by
Rochester, 'Upon Nothing' (1680?). The wit of this poem depends
upon its solemn and protracted pretence that a negative quality is
actually a positive one – just as discernible, just as active. And this
witty game turns out to have an excellent philosophical underpinning; for it is only by distinguishing a positive 'something' from a
negative 'nothing' that we get any purchase upon it, as Rochester
points out:

> Great *Negative*, how vainly wou'd the Wise
> Enquire, define, distinguish, teach, devise,
> Didst thou not stand to point their dull *Philosophies*.

This inversion is delightfully fertile in jokes, as 'something' and
'nothing' skate helplessly between their philosophical and idioma-
tic meanings:

> But *Nothing*, why do's Something still permit
> That Sacred *Monarchs* shou'd at Council sit
> With *persons* highly thought, at best, for *nothing* fit?

> Whil'st weighty *Something* modestly abstains
> From Princes *Coffers*, and from States-mens *Brains*,
> And *Nothing* there, like stately [Something] reigns?

And to end the poem there is the straightforward pleasure of
satirical name-calling, and nihilism:

> *French* Truth, *Dutch* Prowess, *British* Policy,
> *Hybernian* Learning, *Scotch* Civility,
> *Spaniards* Dispatch, *Danes* Wit, are mainly seen in thee.
> The Great *Mans* Gratitude to his best *Friend*,
> *Kings* Promises, *Whores* Vows, towards thee they bend,
> Flow swiftly into thee, and in thee ever end.
>
> (28–30, 37–42, 46–51)

The entire habit of mind revealed by this poem proves deeply
congenial to the young Pope – so much so, that we might say this
solemn pretence that 'nothing' is 'something' becomes the mains-
pring of his satire, from the *Rape of the Lock* to the *Dunciad*. It charms

him as a poet, because the straightforward statement of what he actually believes is poetically inert beside the shimmering paradoxes of what he does not believe: that Belinda's lock of hair is a matter of cosmic concern, or the dullness of the Dunces is worthy of an epic. Inversion does not only lead to greater poetic vitality; by teasing the imagination with a kind of significance which is absurdly disproportionate to its object, it also raises the question of what exactly it is we are laughing at – and whether we ought to be laughing at all. Where does the scope of absurdity end? How do we know that 'something' is ever more than 'nothing'? 'People who would rather it were let alone laugh at it, and seem heartily merry, at the same time that they are uneasy', Pope noted of the *Rape of the Lock*'s first readers; ''tis a sort of writing very like tickling.'[16]

If Rochester can celebrate 'nothing' so elaborately, the young Pope can celebrate 'silence', and its mortal enemy, the word. In this comic version of Genesis, where the word is the great midwife of creation, and Dulness its antagonist still yearning for the primordial silence, we can glimpse what became of the opening vision of the *Dunciad*. This is part of the earliest extant draft (the poem was much revised, before printing in 1712):

Great breathing space! er'e time commenc'd with Earth,
Er'e fruitfull Thought conceived Creations Birth
Or Midwife word gave aid and spake the Infant forth

Opposing Elements against thee joyn'd
And a long Race to break thy sway combin'd,
(Whom Elements compos'd) the Race of human kind

When thought thy captive offspring thou didst free
Whisper a soft Deserter stole from thee
And rebell Speech disturb'd thy Midnight Majesty

Then wanton Sence began abroad to go
And gawdy Science drest himself to shew
And wicked Witt arose thy most abusive foe . . .

With thee in private Modest Dulness lyes
And in thy Bosom lurks in Thoughts disguise
Thou Varnisher of fools, and Cheat of all the Wise

Yet on both sides thy kindness is confest
Folly by thee lyes sleeping in the Breast
And 'tis in thee att last that Wisdom seeks for Rest . . .
                                    (7–18, 25–30)

Once 'silence' becomes an active force, all sorts of witty discoveries follow: that 'Whisper' is a 'soft Deserter', 'Speech' a 'rebell', and 'Silence' itself the possessor of 'Midnight Majesty', or a vast 'Bosom' where 'Modest Dulness' can decently hide itself. These personifications seem to stir into life under the poet's very eyes, and rise up from the page on their own poetic feet; they are a miniature example of the creativity which enables Pope later to bring off a unique success in the *Rape of the Lock*, where he animates a whole new order of supernatural beings, the sylphs, which hover, like silence, between sense and nonsense. The Goddess Dulness in the *Dunciad* is another of these substantially-insubstantial creations, who springs into life as naturally as Silence, in this poem, converts into a deity at the close:

Thou bashfull Goddes stop'st my weak essays
Thou fo[r]cest me too, and whilst my voice I raise
Thou fliest disturbed away and does avoid my Praise.
                                    (46–8)

The satire on Settle and this imitation of Rochester (both from c.1702, when Pope was fourteen) are the clearest indications of the directions in which Pope's powers were growing, and of how tiny suggestions could lie in his mind for decades, till they burst into florid growth like the proverbial mustard seed. But the early production he set most store by and chose to introduce his name to the public was, as we noted above, his *Pastorals*. Doubtless his decision was influenced by the fact that Virgil, too, had begun with writing Eclogues; and that in a genre of elegant make-believe his lack of experience could be more than compensated for by reading and skill. He prepared them for publication with a rigour surprising even for such a conscious perfectionist: they were begun at age sixteen, but not published until he was twenty-one (in 1709), when they could, and did, earn him the praise he was seeking:

He has taken very freely from the Ancients. But what he has mixed of his own with theirs is no way inferior to what he has taken from them. It is not flattery at all to say that Virgil had written nothing so good at his Age.[17]

Pastoral is a genre in which conscious artificiality is a large part of the charm, and what is not said is almost as important as what is. The genre is flagrantly unrelated to actual country living, in which mud sticks, lambs are docked and castrated, and the sight which most gladdens the shepherd's eye is the butcher's van (or its eighteenth-century equivalent): Pope lived in the country and knew this as well as anyone else, but what preoccupies him in these poems is something quite distinct – the literary never-never land created first in Greece by Theocritus, and rediscovered by Virgil in Rome, which is created everywhere that town-cramped imaginations dream of a world not created by man. Pastoral poetry grew up with the first cities, and it has all the charm of an urban park or garden. The urban sensibility turns to it for relief: to breathe the sent of flowers; to mark, with a shade of melancholy, the fragility of their petals, and to notice, with a philosophical pang, how these are tossed and torn by the rough winds of reality.

Pope's *Pastorals*, then, are exquisitely musical celebrations of the lives of shepherds, whose pious, candid minds have never been touched by the anxiety of ring-worm. If a shadow passes over the poetry, it comes from a great distance: the fact of death, which Lycidas laments in *Winter*, or the passage of the seasons, marked by the title of the four poems, which reminds us of the inexorable nature of time. Under the shade of these darker realities, the shepherds are free to carol their passions, and to wager a lamb on the outcome of their song-contests in a style of artful simplicity, as in *Spring*:

> DAPHNIS
> Hear how the Birds, on ev'ry bloomy Spray,
> With joyous Musick wake the dawning Day!
> Why sit we mute, when early Linnets sing,
> When warbling *Philomel* salutes the Spring?
> Why sit we sad, when *Phosphor* shines so clear,
> And lavish Nature paints the Purple Year?
> STREPHON
> Sing then, and *Damon* shall attend the Strain,
> While yon slow Oxen turn the furrow'd Plain.
> Here the bright Crocus and blue Vi'let glow;

> Here Western Winds on breathing Roses blow.
> I'll stake yon' Lamb that near the Fountain plays,
> And from the Brink his dancing Shade surveys.
>   (23–34)

'Artful simplicity' is a very different thing from simplicity, and the reader to whom these verses seem no great achievement may like to consider how often Pope rewrote these lines to make them run so effortlessly, and how carefully he observes the thin line that divides the simple ('innocent, natural') from the simple ('silly'). That he was aware of the danger he ran shows in the mockery he poured on the rival *Pastorals* of Ambrose Philips, who took Spenser rather than Virgil for his model, and relied on what Pope sardonically terms a '*beautiful Rusticity*':

> Ah me the while! ah me! the luckless Day,
> Ah luckless Lad! the rather might I say;
> Ah silly I! more silly than my Sheep,
> Which on the flowry Plains I once did keep.

Pope archly comments,

> How he still Charms the Ear with these artful Repetitions of the Epithets; and how significant is the last Verse! I defy the most common Reader to repeat them, without feeling some Motions of Compassion.[18]

What it takes to 'Charm the Ear' in Pope's view are cadences, rhythms and formulae that have pleased since Virgil's day; poetic stratagems that reunite poetry with the nature of song, and reverberate down from Virgil's 'songs' to the imaginary 'songs' of the shepherds. Such a verse as this (from *Spring*) is in fact a translation from Virgil – as Pope himself points out in a footnote:

> DAMON
> Then sing by turns, by turns the Muses sing,
> Now Hawthorns blossom, now the Daisies spring,
> Now Leaves the Trees, and Flow'rs adorn the Ground;
> Begin, the Vales shall ev'ry Note rebound.
>   (41–4; cf. *Ecl.* III, 55–9)

And though pastoral survives by the rejection of everyday reality, Pope also fathoms its deeper significance, which lies in the imitation of Nature's own processes in poetry. His verse paragraphs unfold themselves as naturally as a flower opens and closes in the sunshine:

> Go gentle Gales, and bear my Sighs away!
> Curs'd be the Fields that cause my *Delia's* Stay:
> Fade ev'ry Blossom, wither ev'ry Tree,
> Dye ev'ry Flow'r, and perish All, but She.
> What have I said? – where-e'er my *Delia* flies,
> Let Spring attend, and sudden Flow'rs arise;
> Let opening Roses knotted Oaks adorn,
> And liquid Amber drop from ev'ry Thorn.
>
> (*Autumn*, 31–8)

We need not be surprised that the *Pastorals* were solicited by the leading publisher of the day on sight,[19] or that when published along with Pope's translation of an episode from Homer and *The Merchant's Tale* from Chaucer, they made some critics ask whether they had a new Virgil in their midst.

2

Out in the World

There followed a series of highly assured poems in a wide variety of forms, by which Pope asserted his claim to be a 'new classic': the *Essay on Criticism* (1711), two versions of the *Rape of the Lock* (1712–14), *Windsor Forest* (1713), the *Temple of Fame* (1715), and *Eloisa to Abelard* – which made its first appearance in the proud young poet's new collection, the *Works* of 1717. At the same time, Pope was making a major translation of Homer's *Iliad*; a work so significant for his literary life, that it deserves a chapter to itself.

This period of prolific activity and mounting fame came at an interesting transition in the history of publishing: the seventeenth-century world of court patronage had passed away, and writers who aimed to make a living by their pen accepted patronage from political factions instead. The more obvious alternative, of making money by selling work directly to the publisher or bookseller (who was usually the same person), was made uneconomic by the way the booksellers contracted for possession of the work entire, and were not obliged to make any extra payment to the author for subsequent editions when the work proved successful – and also by the laxity of the law on copyright, which meant that pirate editions flourished unchecked.

Pope entered this world with two conflicting ambitions. On the one hand, he wished to avoid making 'his talents subservient to the mean and unworthy ends of Party',[1] but on the other, he wished to make a living – the few thousands he had received from his father being largely bound up in annuities, and leaving him (as he later told Spence) 'none – not even to buy books.'[2] The solution he hit upon seems to have been the upshot of a mixture of business instinct and the same creativity that made him a poet: he made his works into a public commodity so desirable that he could make contracts with booksellers on unheard-of terms, and he became to all intents and purposes his own publisher, issuing his works in a variety of formats on varying qualities of paper, and also reissuing them in improved versions of annotation and revision, at great profit to himself. Thus, from the thirteen guineas Pope received for his *Pastorals* and first translations in 1709, we find him contracting in 1714 for an *Iliad* translation that brought him in excess of £5000 (upwards of £125 000 by today's values), and enabled him to live like a country gentleman for the rest of his life.

This determination to create the public that would support him leads to a striking paradox in Pope's literary life. The young poet who has apprenticed himself to the past, whose intimates are Homer and Virgil, Ovid and Horace, is also the canny publicist who is thoroughly at home in the world of piratical booksellers and pamphlet writers. Though his own dealings are with the most reputable booksellers, he keeps abreast of all the reading-matter pouring from the presses, and understands the mechanisms of publicity, scandal and piracy as well as the gutter press does; when the notorious pirate publisher Edmund Curll implicates Pope in the printing of some stolen *Court Poems* (1716), Pope administers him an emetic in a glass of sherry, and not content with a private revenge, celebrates it in a pamphlet, *A Full and True Account of a Horrid and Barbarous Revenge by Poison, On the Body of Mr. Edm. Curll.* And when Curll responds by printing a burlesque of the first psalm, and some early letters of Pope's that he did not in the least intend for publication, the poet replies by incarcerating Curll in the *Dunciad* for all time.

Pope was, in fact, more completely a man of literature than any other writer of the day. His friends Jonathan Swift (1667–1745) and John Gay (1685–1732) were also men of letters, but they looked towards the Church and the Court for a livelihood; Joseph Addison (1672–1719) and Richard Steele (1672–1729) were prolific essayists, but they took government posts and married for ambition. Pope alone found a way of supporting himself by his pen, and he achieved it by mastering the art of publishing from the ground upwards. If his head is in a rarefied atmosphere, communing with Homer, his feet are firmly in the dung-heap (where, he might have riposted, Homer's would have also been, when alive). The hygienic gap we take for granted between the production of verse, and the commercial exploitation of it, did not exist for Pope; and we should not imagine him bending his talent to commercialism with fastidious regret, but with fascination and energy. In the Darwinian jungle that is early publishing, he feels himself thoroughly equipped to survive.

FRIENDS, WOMEN AND LADIES

These years leading up to the first volume of *Works*, when the poet
was in his twenties, were the busiest and most sociable of Pope's
life. In the country, his circle consisted of the Catholic gentry,
including the Blount family (whose daughters he courted with
varying degrees of seriousness) and the Carylls, through whose
intervention he commemorated the quarrel between two other
Catholic families, the Petres and the Fermors, in the *Rape of the Lock*.
In London, he was adopted by both Whigs like Addison and Steele
(for whom he wrote various essays and occasional poems), and
Tories, like Swift. Though Pope never committed himself to either
party, it was with the Tories he was most associated and who
proved his most lasting friends, in particular the group centred on
the ministry of Lords Oxford and Bolingbroke during the last years
of Queen Anne: Jonathan Swift, Archdeacon Thomas Parnell
(1679–1718), Bishop Francis Atterbury (1662–1732), and Dr John
Arbuthnot (1667–1735), the Queen's physician. With these genial
and subversive friends – their sense of humour not at all impaired
by their connections with the church – and John Gay, Pope
founded the 'Scriblerus Club', where the group contributed from
their various professional perspectives to the facetious memoir of a
learned fool, Martinus Scriblerus, who had 'dipped in every art
and science, but injudiciously in each.'[3] Nothing amused them
more than the spectacle of learning misapplied, and the leaden
scholarly instinct that converts knowledge to lumber to keep it
quiescent; the short-term results of the club were a series of merry
dinners, and the long-term results, the satire on pedantry in
Gulliver's Travels, Pope's mock-treatise, *The Art of Sinking in Poetry*,
and his *Dunciad*, annotated by Martinus Scriblerus himself. We can
catch the true 'Scriblerian Manner', and the tone of those dinners,
in the epigram Pope and Parnell composed on a misty ride to visit
Swift in 1714:

> How foolish Men on Expeditions goe!
> Unweeting Wantons of their wetting Woe!
> For drizling Damps descend adown the Plain
> And seem a thicker Dew, or thinner Rain;
> Yet Dew or Rain may wett us to the Shift,
> We'll not be slow to visit Dr. Swift.[4]

It is easy to forget, in scanning the productiveness and sociability of this period of Pope's life, that its apparent normality was a pretence, sustained in the teeth of deformity and pain. His childhood tuberculosis of the bone (Pott's Disease) had arrested his height at 4'6" and weakened and curved his spine, affecting respiration, digestion and the heart; if he stayed up carousing with his healthy friends it was at the risk of undermining his fragile constitution, and if he persisted in 'the life of a Wit', which he knew to be 'a warfare upon earth', it was at the risk of being called a 'hunch-back'd Toad' by anyone he angered of normal height.[5] The fact that he contrived to live as if perfectly equipped for the cruelties of eighteenth-century public life, and to persuade all except his enemies to ignore his deformity, is a tribute to Pope's power over others' imaginations, and the distance he himself maintained between his spirit and the 'crazy Carcass' which housed it.

In his relations with women, however, his shape was a factor to make him distinguish sharply between 'women', who laughed, and 'ladies', who did not. (He refers to himself wryly in a letter as 'that little Alexander the women laugh at'.)[6] His friendships with women have a kind of high-wire tension, where his sense of humour and the clear impossibility of his being accepted for a lover supply the elegance, and the reality of his passion supplies the danger, of the performance. At no time is there any question of marriage, but the acuteness of his intuitions about women, and the sharpness of frustration, lead to friendships that are always kindling into something else – before they break off; as with the witty poetess, Lady Mary Wortley Montagu (1689–1762), and Teresa Blount. His need to love, educate, and protect, was most lastingly focused on Teresa's younger sister Martha, however, who responded gratefully with a lifetime's devotion. Whether she was ever Pope's mistress is doubtful, but she was the object of the century's finest poetical compliment (the *Epistle to a Lady*), and the chief beneficiary of his will.

THE COLLECTED *WORKS* OF 1717

One of the most interesting aspects of human development is its tendency to go in circles – always returning to the place it started from, though the journey is made from increasingly distant points on the map. This is supremely true of artists, whose work to the discerning eye is always the same piece of work, in a differing stage of development. It is as if the artist had a template within, which he cannot abandon even if he wants to; and though this sounds like a limitation, it is one of those limitations that makes everything else possible. Having found his template, the artist learns how to make it subsume more meaning, how to condense more implications into his form; and by going in circles, he ends in a place very far from his starting point – though it is also that, as well.

The is particularly true of Pope, whose poems go in ever-widening circles from the juvenilia we have seen, to the last revision of the *Dunciad*. The template is not a commitment to one particular genre, but to the simultaneous exploration of many, which enables him to capture conflicting aspects of reality and to exploit the many facets of his nature. The secret of this variety is an exquisite sense of what belongs in each kind of poetry – what the age called 'decorum' – and a rigorous exclusion of all else. The poems, however apparently contradictory in tone and philosophy, are each being played by the rules of the game.

The 'second circle' of Pope's development shows the *Pastorals* growing into a topographical celebration of country life, *Windsor Forest*, the early translation of Ovid's love letter, *Sapho to Phaon*, growing into *Eloisa to Abelard*, the mock-epic gifts and inverted metaphors of Pope's Dorset and Rochester imitations developing into the *Rape of the Lock*, and Pope mastering two forms he has not attempted before: the verse essay (*An Essay on Criticism*) and the elegy (*Elegy to the Memory of an Unfortunate Lady*). What lay behind this second round of creativity was not only increasing skill as a poet, but a new mental clarity and organisation. Pope seems to have felt that his happy but haphazard education, in which he found his own way through the classics and picked up languages as he went, needed severe discipline in order to bear fruit; and he regarded himself in later life as someone who had 'done' his education twice over. The friend and co-editor of Pope's old age, Warburton, phrases it like this:

At twenty, when the impetuosity of his spirits began to suffer his genius to be put under restraint, he went over all the parts of his education a-new, from the very beginning, and in a regular, and more artful manner. He penetrated into the general grounds and reasons of speech; he learnt to distinguish the several species of style; he studied the peculiar genius and character of each language; he reduced his natural talent for poetry to a science, and mastered those parts of philosophy that would most contribute to enrich his vein. And all this, with such continued attention, labour, and severity that he used to say, he had been seven years (that is, from twenty to twenty-seven) in unlearning all he had been acquiring for twice seven.[7]

AN ESSAY ON CRITICISM

The plainest fruit of this is the *Essay on Criticism* (published 1711), a work of astonishing maturity for a poet of twenty-three, and which (says Johnson),

> displays such extent of comprehension, such nicety of distinction, such acquaintance with mankind, and such knowledge both of ancient and modern learning as are not often attained by the maturest age and longest experience.[8]

Subsumed in this verse essay are ideas from all the major Greek, Roman and Renaissance treatises on how to read, and how to write, as well as a considerable amount of reading in French criticism, and a familiarity with the famous English essays of the Restoration, Roscommon's *Essay on Translated Verse* (1684) and Mulgrave's *Essay upon Poetry* (1682). What is striking, however, is not the display of knowledge, but the unhampered assurance of this latest contribution to the long debate. Other theoreticians are earnest, manly, wise – Pope is scintillating, swift, and comic: he passes rapidly from theory to illustration, and sketches a few contemporary portraits on the way, while proverbs spin off from his pen to lead an independent existence of their own ('A *little Learning* is a dang'rous Thing', 'For *Fools* rush in where *Angels* fear to tread', 'To Err is *Humane*; to Forgive, *Divine*.') This vitality is what cannot be imitated, or acquired; it is the result of intelligence happily engaged with vital ideas that are closely associated with the nature of intelligence itself. Nor can proverbs be coined by anyone who tries; words only form themselves into natural, irresistible phrases for the writer who has embedded himself in the language, and can imitate its processes. If this is a work of staggering precocity, we can nonetheless say that Pope has been working at it for nearly twenty years, since childhood:

> True Ease in Writing comes from Art, not Chance,
> As those move easiest who have learn'd to dance.
>
> (362–3)

Why does criticism need an essay at all, we may wonder? Because it involves the exercise of judgement. The fine poise of our faculties that makes judgement possible is really a synonym for intelligence, and what Pope is discussing here is the proper use of the human mind. A bad poet merely makes us yawn, but a bad critic makes us more stupid:

> 'Tis hard to say, if greater Want of Skill
> Appear in *Writing* or in *Judging* ill;
> But, of the two, less dang'rous is th' Offence,
> To tire our *Patience*, than mislead our *Sense*.
>
> (1–4)

Why is the good critic such a rarity? What is it that interferes with human judgement? The problem lies in human quiddity:

> 'Tis with our *Judgements* as our *Watches*, none
> Go just *alike*, yet each believes his own.
>
> (9–10)

None of us can be dissuaded from 'trusting our own watch', and it is proper that we should – but we must be all the more cautious to observe how our judgement is formed. The first task of the critic is self-knowledge, the ability to assess the value of his own opinion:

> Be sure *your self* and your own *Reach* to know,
> How far your *Genius*, *Taste*, and *Learning* go;
> Launch not beyond your Depth, but be discreet,
> And mark *that Point* where Sense and Dulness *meet*.
>
> (48–51)

But something else usually intervenes, to save us from the painful effort of self-knowledge:

Of all the Causes which conspire to blind
Man's erring Judgment, and misguide the Mind,
What the weak Head with strongest Byass rules,
Is *Pride*, the *never-failing Vice of Fools.*
Whatever Nature has in *Worth* deny'd,
She gives in large Recruits of *needful Pride;*
For as in *Bodies*, thus in *Souls*, we find
What wants in *Blood* and *Spirits*, swell'd with *Wind;*
Pride, where Wit fails, steps in to our Defence,
And fills up all the *mighty Void* of *Sense!*
If once right Reason drives *that Cloud* away,
Truth breaks upon us with *resistless Day;*
Trust not your self; but your Defects to know,
Make use of ev'ry *Friend* – and ev'ry *Foe.*

(201–14)

It is pride that covers our nakedness, and makes us so determined to believe our own 'watch' rather than another's. This is the point at which proper self-reliance becomes mere complacency – and where we only become better critics by being better people. The key term here is 'right Reason', a faculty that for Pope is both ethical and rational: not only our power of thinking, but our power of locating ourselves rightly in the universe, so that we see ourselves in true perspective. Once we chase the clouds of egotistical pride off our horizons, '*Truth* breaks upon us with *resistless Day*'; and it is an article of faith in Pope's philosophy that the light is irresistible: we recognise it, and delight in it, at the same moment.

This is the first formulation of an idea that underlies Pope's poetry for the rest of his life: that Reason leads directly to a grasp of Nature ('the working of the whole'), or it is not worthy of the name. Just as our individual watches bear an ascertainable relation to the movement of the sun, and can be adjusted to reflect it more accurately still, so our individual judgements can be brought into closer relation with the truth, if we only keep our eye on the light. Hence his central advice to the critic:

First follow NATURE, and your Judgment frame
By her just Standard, which is still the same:
Unerring Nature, still divinely bright,

> One *clear*, *unchang'd*, and *Universal* Light,
> Life, Force, and Beauty, must to all impart,
> At once the *Source*, and *End*, and *Test* of *Art*.
> (68–73)

Every true act of critical judgement is in accord with Nature,
uncovering the Nature in the work it judges. God, in this scheme
of things, is the first artist, whose creation is the whole of Nature;
the artist imitates him, recreating Nature in a smaller compass; and
the critic celebrates the connection between them both. Hence the
immense value Pope places on 'right Reason', which understands
and accepts the workings of Nature – which understands, indeed,
that it is itself a piece of that whole. And hence also Pope's
assumption that an error in criticism is a serious thing, for it is a
miniature Fall that leaves the critic at odds with truth and Nature.

It is not only pride that the critic must be alert to; it may also be
the effects of a shallow education,

> A *little Learning* is a dang'rous Thing;
> Drink deep, or taste not the *Pierian* Spring,
> (215–16)

prejudice,

> Some judge of Authors' *Names*, not *Works*, and then
> Nor praise nor blame the *Writings*, but the *Men*,
> (412–13)

fashion,

> Some praise at Morning what they blame at Night;
> But always think the *last* Opinion *right*,
> (430–31)

modernist conceit,

> *We* think our *Fathers* Fools, so *wise* we grow;
> Our *wiser Sons*, no doubt, will think *us* so,
> (438–9)

or jealousy,

> Each burns alike, who can, or cannot write,
> Or with a *rival*'s, or an *Eunuch*'s spite.
> (30–31)

Above all, the critic should be wary of praising a work merely for its conformity to the 'Rules' derived from the practice of Greece and Rome. If a writer successfully takes the licence of pleasing us in a new way, '*that Licence is a Rule*':

> Great Wits sometimes may *gloriously offend*,
> And *rise* to *Faults* true Criticks *dare not mend*;
> From *vulgar Bounds* with *brave Disorder* part,
> And *snatch* a *Grace* beyond the reach of Art,
> Which, without passing thro' the *Judgment*, gains
> The *Heart*, and all its End *at once* attains.
> (152–7)

This is not, of course, to say that Pope is lacking in reverence for these rules; but he does not accept them as the crippling prescriptions for the creation of art which so many of his contemporaries took them to be. They are perceptions, rather, about the way art works, as 'natural' as the laws of physics, which explain the workings of the physical universe:

> Those RULES of old *discover'd*, not *devis'd*,
> Are *Nature* still, but *Nature Methodiz'd*;
> *Nature*, like *Liberty*, is but restrain'd
> By the same Laws which first *herself* ordain'd.
> (88–91)

The essay form is flexible enough to illustrate this by a digression on the 'rules' for the heroic couplet – on which Pope's own are an entertaining commentary. While Pope's own manner is 'Nature Methodiz'd', a style of conversation that slips naturally into couplet form, he knows how rarely the couplet's innate weaknesses are avoided: its repetitious rhymes,

> Where-e'er you find *the cooling Western Breeze*,
> In the next Line, it *whispers thro' the Trees*;

> If *Chrystal Streams with pleasing Murmurs creep,*
> The Reader's threaten'd (not in vain) with *Sleep,*
> (350–53)

and the little words the poet relies on for padding, which rob the
line of rhythm and energy,

> While *Expletives* their feeble Aid *do* join
> And ten low Words oft creep in one dull Line.
> (346–7)

What Pope loves in the couplet is its 'Easie Vigor' – the elegance
founded in muscular strength that every dancer possesses:

> True Ease in Writing comes from Art, not Chance,
> As those move easiest who have learn'd to dance.
> (362–3)

And he loves the elasticity of its rhythm which, well-handled, can
imitate ponderous effort or effortless lightness:

> When *Ajax* strives, some Rock's vast Weight to throw,
> The Line too *labours*, and the Words move *slow*;
> Not so, when swift *Camilla* scours the Plain,
> Flies o'er th'unbending Corn and skims along the Main.
> (370–73)

This is his famous doctrine of imitation, 'The *Sound* must seem an
Eccho to the *Sense*' (365), at which he laboured all his life (and much
oftener, he feelingly remarked, 'than anyone minds it').[9]
     The true critic is the man whose taste in these matters is as just
as his reason is clear; a man whose heart and brain are equally at
one with Nature. It follows, as Pope was to reiterate for the rest of
his life, that the well-judging man is also a good man – and a critic
the man one would choose for a friend:

> But where's the Man, who Counsel *can* bestow,
> Still *pleas'd* to *teach*, and yet not *proud to know?* . . .
> Tho' Learn'd, well-bred; and tho' well-bred, sincere;
> Modestly bold, and Humanly severe?
> Who to a *Friend* his Faults can freely show,

And gladly praise the Merit of a *Foe*?
Blest with a *Taste* exact, yet unconfin'd;
A *Knowledge* both of *Books* and *Humankind*;
Gen'rous *Converse*; a *Soul* exempt from *Pride*,
And *Love* to *Praise*, with *Reason* on his Side?
                    (631–2, 635–42)

THE *RAPE OF THE LOCK*

There is as much reading, though of a different kind, submerged in the *Rape of the Lock*; indeed, nothing Pope ever wrote had more poetical 'parents' than this mock epic, which has won him more admirers in every age than any other of his poems. But if, as noted above, literature must always resemble other literature more than it resembles anything else, a new work may sum up and perfect many past ones without being derivative; and Pope's mock-epic is the most brilliant contribution to a long series of games that was being played with the tone and structure of epic.

The original stimulus to gaiety was the nature of epic itself. It is so very high-toned, so remorselessly serious about man and his destiny, that it defies the reader to remember that, if man is capable of being large, he is also capable of being very small – and if his destiny matters, he is often more concerned with the nature of his dinner. Thus, the language of epic can easily detach itself from felt reality: a discrepancy that was exploited in Greek literature itself, when the language of Homer was later used to describe a ludicrous 'battle' between an army of frogs and mice (the *Batrachomyomachia*). Wherever the *Iliad* or the *Aeneid* were highly valued, they generated such comic imitations, by a kind of reflex: in Italy, for instance, Tassoni produced *La Secchia Rapita* (*The Rape of the Bucket*, 1622), in which the citizens of Bologna and Modena fight over the theft of a bucket, and squabble in a mixture of heroic diction and broad dialect; and in France, Boileau produced the celebrated mock-epic *Le Lutrin* (*The Lectern*, 1674) about a provincial quarrel over the placing of a lectern in a church. The most recent example in England was the work of Pope's friend, the genial and literary doctor, Samuel Garth, who had burlesqued a contemporary dispute between doctors and apothecaries over drug-dispensing rights in *The Dispensary* (1699).

What these poems had in common, and had made *de rigueur* for the game by the time Pope joined it, was sustained allusion to the *Iliad*, the *Odyssey*, and even more frequently, the *Aeneid*. The allusion was not just a matter of style, but of famous speeches, significant episodes, and allegorical figures, like Fame. What begins as broad fun in Tassoni – the captains addressing their troops in dialect, so a contemporary voice breaks through the heroic façade – becomes an exquisite manipulation of parallels in Boileau, where a hairdresser's wife, abandoned for the night, addresses her husband in the plangent tones of Dido, seduced and abandoned by Aeneas. In *The Dispensary*, Garth imitates the whole of *Aeneid* Book VI, the hero's journey through the underworld of the dead, which becomes a physician's painful encounter with the shades of dead colleagues, ex-patients, and his ruined mistress – who firmly snubs him, just as the ghost of Dido snubbed Aeneas.

Very little in the mock-epic is Pope's invention, then; what is his own is the depth of the joke, and the implications he teases out from the ambiguity of the form. The mock-epic, in Pope's conception, has very little to do with mockery: it returns us to the giddy inversions of 'Upon Nothing', and the question of how we ever know for sure that 'something' is not 'nothing'. If little things are described in large words, are they little – or large? This is the 'writing like tickling' that makes us half-wish the poet would stop, and very uncertain where our laughter will end.

What is also uniquely Pope's is the coherence of the surface of the poem, so that the everyday world of the action is not constantly poking through the heroic pretence and destroying the illusion, as in *The Dispensary*. And he also chooses his subject with finer discrimination than previous practitioners. Boileau's lectern, for instance, is the focus for some serious thoughts about the disparity between the church's spiritual and worldly faces, but it is not in itself a poetical object; and the quarrel between the opposing factions takes place, somewhat irrelevantly, in a bookshop. Pope's subject, the loss of a lock of Arabella Fermor's hair to a suitor, touches off much wider reverberations. One severance being a kind of shadow-play of another, we are made to think of the loss of her virginity; and also of the ambiguity of the word 'rape' in heroic poetry – as in the 'Rape of Helen', who did not put up any great resistance.[10] The lock is lovely, irreplaceable, valueless and invaluable – and hence a proper focus for the conflicting and ambiguous feelings of the period about women's virginity.

Pope's best stroke, technically speaking, is his invention of a new mock-epic 'machinery' to take the place of the gods of epic: the sylphs and gnomes that watch over the heroine's destiny. When he first wrote the poem in 1712, it was in two cantos only, without this extra dimension; but once he realised what an opportunity he had missed, he expanded it into five (1714), and viewed the seamless end product with unbounded satisfaction. ('All the machinery, you know, was added afterwards, and the making that and what was published before hit so well together, is I think one of the greatest proofs of judgement of anything I ever did,' he later told Spence.)[11] Boileau and Garth had personified Law and Piety, Health and Sloth, but these were allegorical figures to inspire activity in others, not independent powers with a life of their own. It was Pope who uncovered the real secret of epic 'machinery': the gods must be both involved in, and detached from, the world of men – detached by force of their immortality, but involved by their identification with human greatness. Because they 'adopt' human concerns of their own free will, they stimulate our imaginations to magnify these things also, and to conceive of what so involves the gods as lying on the largest scale of significance. (As Pope archly explains to Arabella Fermor, 'The ancient Poets are in one respect like many modern Ladies; Let an Action be never so trivial in it self, they always make it appear of the utmost Importance', and the 'machinery' is what effects this.)[12]

The sylphs and gnomes are, of course, absurdly miniature forms of divinity; but even miniaturised, they retain their power to magnify. Johnson expresses the delight in their activity few readers fail to share:

In this work are exhibited in a very high degree the two most engaging powers of an author: new things are made familiar, and familiar things are made new. A race of aerial people never heard of before is presented to us in a manner so clear and easy, that the reader seeks for no further information, but immediately mingles with his new acquaintance, adopts their interests and attends their pursuits, loves a Sylph, and detests a Gnome.

That familiar things are made new every paragraph will prove. The subject of the poem is an event below the common incidents of common life; nothing real is introduced that is not seen so often as to be no longer regarded, yet the whole detail of a female-day is here brought before us, invested with so much art of decoration that, though nothing is disguised, every thing is striking, and we feel all the appetite of curiosity for that from which we have a thousand times turned fastidiously away.[13]

'Though nothing is disguised, every thing is striking': far from being a mere addition to the poem, the spirits embody its meaning, for they can only be visible to mortals on condition of 'an inviolate Preservation of Chastity', as Pope slyly mentions in the Dedication.[14] They are Belinda's fragile condition made strikingly visible, and their dual nature embodies the paradoxical nature of chastity in female experience. The sylphs are virginity in the marriage market: worldly and coy, timid and alluring; the gnomes are virginity on the shelf, splenetic and glum, hypocritical and fierce.

Much of the satire of the poem is lavished on what Johnson calls 'the whole detail of a female-day' – the preoccupation with rouge and eyedrops, flounces and furbelows, which marks the society belle. But with the additional presence of the rainbow-coloured sylphs, the ironies coruscate and spread in myriad directions to colour the absurdity of Belinda's predicament, as well as her behaviour. The sylphs, we are told, were all coquettes in their earthly incarnation, and as spirits they are supremely concerned with the heroine's good name – as is the coquette, of course, in a world where a single rumour can send her market-price tumbling. ('All your Honour in a Whisper lost!' as Thalestris says (IV, 110).) There is a delightful parallel with the epic hero's obsession with his 'Fame'; but the connection points a difference, too, for what the hero earns by action, the contemporary heroine must earn by inaction, under the most tempting possible circumstances. She must withhold herself from all the opportunities presented by the balls and masquerades at which her beauty is placed on show, and resist not only the tempter without, but the tempter within, her own 'melting' nature:

> What guards the Purity of melting Maids,
> In Courtly Balls, and Midnight Masquerades,
> Safe from the treach'rous Friend, the daring Spark,
> The Glance by Day, the Whisper in the Dark;
> When kind Occasion prompts their warm Desires,
> When Musick softens, and when Dancing fires?
> 'Tis but their *Sylph*, the wise Celestials know,
> Tho' *Honour* is the Word with Men below.
>
>   (I, 71–8)

The paradoxical unnaturalness of her predicament – obliged to be on guard against what nature most naturally prompts, and what she is publicly considered to know nothing about – is emphasised by the great distinction between the sylphs and Belinda. For they retain their 'Honour' so firmly by being made of air, while Belinda has a body; and her unwelcome choice as a woman is between exploiting her sexuality without compromising herself, like the sylphs, or suppressing its claims and turning prude, as the gnomes have done.

The airy disembodiment of the sylphs is Pope's exquisite substitution for the immortality of Homer's gods, and just as the most poignant moments of the *Iliad* occur when the immortals look down on their favourite mortals and realise that, much as they might love them, they cannot save them from death, so the climax of his mock-epic comes when Ariel realises that he cannot protect Belinda from the violation of her lock. The Baron borrows a pair of scissors from Clarissa, and approaches the back of her neck as she innocently bends over her coffee cup:

> He takes the Gift with rev'rence, and extends
> The little Engine on his Fingers' Ends,
> This just behind *Belinda's* Neck he spread,
> As o'er the fragrant Steams she bends her Head:
> Swift to the Lock a thousand Sprights repair,
> A thousand Wings, by turns, blow back the Hair,
> And thrice they twitch'd the Diamond in her Ear,
> Thrice she look'd back, and thrice the Foe drew near.
> Just at that instant, anxious *Ariel* sought
> The close Recesses of the Virgin's Thought;
> As on the Nosegay in her Breast reclin'd,
> He watch'd th' Ideas rising in her Mind,
> Sudden he view'd, in spite of all her Art,
> An Earthly Lover lurking at her Heart.
> Amaz'd, confus'd, he found his Pow'r expir'd,
> Resign'd to Fate, and with a Sigh retir'd.
>   The Peer now spreads the glitt'ring *Forfex* wide,
> T'inclose the Lock; now joins it, to divide.
> Ev'n then, before the fatal Engine clos'd,
> A Wretched *Sylph* too fondly interpos'd;
> Fate urg'd the Sheers, and cut the *Sylph* in twain,
> (But Airy Substance soon unites again)

> The meeting Points the sacred Hair dissever
> From the fair Head, for ever and for ever!
> (III, 131–54)

At the fatal meeting of the scissors is also the exquisite intersection of Belinda's concerns and the sylphs'. They inhabit a realm of disembodied chastity – she has 'an Earthly Lover lurking at her Heart'. (She *is* interested in the Baron, in spite of appearances.) Their pains and losses are ephemeral ('Airy Substance soon unites again') – hers are permanent (the hairs 'dissever/From the fair Head, for ever and for ever!'). The sylphs, like Homer's gods, are a kind of wishful fantasy of what human life might be without human penalties – if it kept all its sweetness, but had its sting removed. The gods and goddesses of Olympus are like men and women in almost every way, save that they never die; and the sylphs have all the charm and beauty of Belinda, except that they never have to cross the line from sexual inexperience to maturity. When Ariel finds Belinda is willing to do so, his power abruptly terminates:

> Amaz'd, confus'd, he found his Pow'r expir'd,
> Resign'd to Fate, and with a Sigh retir'd.

The teasing ambiguity at the heart of the poem is that, while Homer's immortals express for us the pathos of human mortality, Ariel's 'Sigh' at the prospect of Belinda's sexual maturity can hardly be ours – unless we wish to trap her in virginity for ever. But while the poet is hinting that he has as life-and-death a subject for his mock-epic as epic itself, he shows us his heroine steadfastly refusing to behave like one. Her predicament may be worthy of heroic treatment, but her response is as trivial as mock-epic can make it:

> For ever curs'd be this detested Day,
> Which snatch'd my best, my fav'rite Curl away!
> Happy! ah ten times happy, had I been,
> If *Hampton-Court* these Eyes had never seen!
> Yet am not I the first mistaken Maid,
> By Love of *Courts* to num'rous Ills betray'd.
> Oh had I rather un-admir'd remain'd
> In some lone Isle, or distant *Northern* Land;

Where the gilt *Chariot* never marks the Way,
Where none learn *Ombre*, none e'er taste *Bohea*!
There kept my Charms conceal'd from mortal Eye,
Like Roses that in Desarts bloom and die.
What mov'd my Mind with youthful Lords to rome?
O had I stay'd, and said my Pray'rs at home!
'Twas this, the Morning *Omens* seem'd to tell;
Thrice from my trembling hand the *Patch-box* fell;
The tott'ring *China* shook without a Wind,
Nay, *Poll* sat mute, and *Shock* was most Unkind! . . .
See the poor Remnants of these slighted Hairs!
My hands shall rend what ev'n thy Rapine spares: . . .
Oh hadst thou, Cruel! been content to seize
Hairs less in sight, or any Hairs but these!
                    (V, 147–64, 167–8, 175–6)

Belinda's last *double-entendre* conveys even better than her despair,
how little she attends to the sub-text of the poem, and how fully
she shares the moral perspective of the sylphs. 'Honour' is a matter
of social appearances, as the horror of Thalestris beautifully
betrays:

> Gods! shall the Ravisher display your Hair,
> While the Fops envy, and the Ladies stare!
> *Honour* forbid! at whose unrival'd Shrine
> Ease, Pleasure, Virtue, All, our Sex resign.
>   (IV, 103–6)

In a world where 'Virtue' is a small sacrifice to make to 'Honour',
Belinda really has no other recourse than to hysterics for this
'Rapine' of her good name. But before the action collapses into a
burlesque battle of the sexes, and the women relieve their aggression with bodkins and fans, Pope gives us one glimpse of what it
would be to live differently from this: to have internalised one's
sense of 'Honour' where no whisper could hurt it. He transposes
the most famous of all speeches in the *Iliad* into the language of a
coquette, and in the finest serio-comic stroke of the poem, suggests
that the truest form of heroism in this world of social peril would
be – to develop good humour.

   In the Homeric original, a Trojan hero, Sarpedon, is asking the
most radical question possible in the world of epic: why is it he

fights at the forefront of the army, where he is most likely to be killed? And the answer he gives became the classic formulation of the aristocratic code: in peacetime he receives all the privileges of a chief, which must now be justified by his behaviour in battle. It is impossible, in any case, to avoid death in the course of living; and he prefers to give his life away now, when death will bring honour, to losing his life meaninglessly. If we substitute the privilege of great beauty for heroic strength and status, we have the speech of Clarissa (which Pope added in 1717, 'to open more clearly the MORAL of the Poem'):[15]

> Say, why are Beauties prais'd and honour'd most,
> The wise Man's Passion, and the vain Man's Toast?
> Why deck'd with all that Land and Sea afford,
> Why Angels call'd, and Angel-like ador'd?
> Why round our Coaches crowd the white-glov'd Beaus,
> Why bows the Side-box from its inmost Rows?
> How vain are all these Glories, all our Pains,
> Unless good Sense preserve what Beauty gains:
> That Men may say, when we the Front-box grace,
> Behold the first in Virtue, as in Face!
> Oh! if to dance all Night, and dress all Day,
> Charm'd the Small-pox, or chas'd old Age away;
> Who would not scorn what Huswife's Cares produce,
> Or who would learn one earthly Thing of Use?
> To patch, nay ogle, might become a Saint,
> Nor could it sure be such a Sin to paint.
> But since, alas! frail Beauty must decay,
> Curl'd or uncurl'd, since Locks will turn to grey,
> Since painted, or not painted, all shall fade,
> And she who scorns a Man, must die a Maid;
> What then remains, but well our Pow'r to use,
> And keep good Humour still whate'er we lose?
> And trust me, Dear! good Humour can prevail,
> When Airs, and Flights, and Screams, and Scolding fail.
> Beauties in vain their pretty Eyes may roll;
> Charms strike the Sight, but Merit wins the Soul.
>
>   (V, 9–34)

Such excellent advice meets its common fate:

> So spoke the Dame, but no Applause ensu'd;
> *Belinda* frown'd, *Thalestris* call'd her Prude.
>
> (V, 35–6)

But the poet expects us to understand what Belinda spurns – the fact that 'good Humour', like its related faculty, Reason, is the way to maintain ourselves in a right relation with the world around us. This potentially weighty moral, however, is adapted to the scale of the poem and given a novel twist, by being placed in the mouth of a coquette. Just as Sarpedon admits that if he thought he could live for ever, he would certainly not be fighting at Troy, so Clarissa makes it clear that there would be no need for sense or good humour if the fragile world of beauty were permanent: if 'dancing all Night and dressing all Day' could prevent the smallpox and old age,

> Who would not scorn what Huswife's Cares produce,
> Or who would learn one earthly Thing of Use?

It is because Pope admits the attraction of the case for eternal gaiety, a case to which the heroic diction of the poem lends such splendour, that his moral emerges under the pressure of ambiguity and is held taut between the seductive dream of not being serious – and the certainty that death and disease will finally make us so, whatever our feelings in the matter. 'Mock-epic' at this level of ambiguity is hardly to be distinguished from epic, which is also about the difference between the way mortals wish to live, and the way they must. Since Pope here describes an epic choice in the world he actually inhabited, we may wonder whether the *Rape of the Lock* is not, after all, his eighteenth-century epic: miniaturised, inverted, but still the profoundest of meditations on what it means to be human. Certainly the last lines of the poem, after Belinda's lock has risen to heaven as a comet, would need little adjustment to take their place at the end of an *Iliad*:

> Then cease, bright Nymph! to mourn thy ravish'd Hair
> Which adds new Glory to the shining Sphere!
> Not all the Tresses that fair Head can boast
> Shall draw such Envy as the Lock you lost.

For, after all the Murders of your Eye,
When, after Millions slain, your self shall die;
When those fair Suns shall sett, as sett they must,
And all those Tresses shall be laid in Dust;
This Lock, the Muse shall consecrate to Fame,
And mid'st the Stars inscribe *Belinda*'s Name!

                                              (V, 141–50)

ELOISA TO ABELARD

The third poem of this period in which Pope shows himself both
deeply indebted to the past, and freely original, is the heroic epistle
Eloisa to Abelard. It is also one of the rare poems which allows us to
make a guess at the correlation between his life and his poetry –
though, as we should expect with such a conscious artist, the guess
is never confirmed by Pope. What we may say with some assurance is that a powerful poem about sexual frustration could never
have been written by someone who had not experienced it, and the
interrelation between passion and the imagination is grasped in
this poem with astonishing subtlety. We also have Pope's own
oblique comment on the poem's fervour: 'The Epistle of Eloise
grows warm, and begins to have some Breathings of the Heart in it,
which may make posterity think I was in love.'[16] But close
comparisons between Eloisa and Pope will not carry us far – and
even the assumption that the poem sprang out of a hopeless
passion for Lady Mary Wortley Montagu, absent in Turkey
(ll.361–2), must take account of the fact that Pope seems earlier to
have intended the poem to end with a reference to Martha
Blount.[17]

What we know for sure is that Pope conceived the poem on the
model of Ovid's *Heroides* (c.AD 10), soon after the appearance of a
translation of the correspondence between the historical Heloise
and Abelard (by John Hughes, 1713). The fascination of the
Heroides ('Heroines') lay in their indiscretion: Ovid had the idea of
writing verse epistles in the person of various fictional heroines of
antiquity, to explore what Fleet Street (with a similar appetite for
'true confessions') would call 'the woman's view'. Thus Dido
abandoned by Aeneas, Medea wronged by Jason, and Sappho
betrayed by Phaon, all confess themselves on paper, and express
their tumultuous passions with all the more violence because they

have no other outlet; and since, in most cases, they are on the brink of suicide, these are the last words they will ever utter. The fact that the delinquent lover is not there to hear them draws the reader into a peculiarly intimate relation with the heroine. We listen and sympathise the more acutely because, so the letter implies, she can reach no ear but ours.

The adaptation of the Ovidian epistle to the famous story of Heloise (Eloisa) was a poetical *coup* that delighted Pope's contemporaries. Johnson, not given to wholehearted approval, calls the epistle 'one of the most happy productions of human wit: the subject is so judiciously chosen that it would be difficult, in turning over the annals of the world, to find another which so many circumstances concur to recommend.'[18] Eloisa's story has the advantage over its Roman models that it is actually true. She did write letters to Abelard after the violent end of their famous love-affair, which consigned her to a nunnery and Abelard (castrated by her guardian) to the monastery of the Paraclete. The factual background also removes the hint of facetiousness that clings to Ovid's letters – did Dido really have time to pen her reproaches with Aeneas's sword in her lap? – and dignifies the confession: Eloisa is no lachrymose victim of seduction, but a learned abbess, once the pupil as well as lover of the most daring of twelfth-century scholars.

There were other aspects of the story 'concurring to recommend' it: not least, the extreme contrasts it afforded, between past and present, feeling and constraint, and the claims of the soul and body. Ovid's heroines are often trapped by their fate, but none of them is as powerless as Eloisa, whose passion is interdicted by both God and Nature: Abelard is not merely a monk, he is emasculated. And when Ovid underlines the tension between fate and feeling, it is usually at the price of becoming intrusively paradoxical: 'He is frequently witty out of season',[19] admits Dryden, who nonetheless translated three of the epistles, including Dido's (1680), with less-than-seasonable wit:

> Death holds my pen, and dictates what I say,
> While cross my lap thy *Trojan* Sword I lay.
> My tears flow down; the sharp edge cuts their flood,
> And drinks my sorrows, that must drink my blood.
> How well thy gift does with my Fate agree!
> My Funeral pomp is cheaply made by thee.

To no new wounds my bosom I display:
The Sword but enters where Love made the way.
(197–204)

There is abundant paradox in Pope's poem, too but now it is not
a matter of verbal conceits but human feeling – the paradox of
conflicting guilt and passion:

I view my crime, but kindle at the view,
Repent old pleasures, and sollicit new:
Now turn'd to heav'n, I weep my past offence,
Now think of thee, and curse my innocence.
Of all affliction taught a lover yet,
'Tis sure the hardest science to forget!
How shall I lose the sin, yet keep the sense,
And love th' offender, yet detest th' offence?
How the dear object from the crime remove,
Or how distinguish penitence from love?
Unequal task! a passion to resign,
For hearts so touch'd, so pierc'd, so lost as mine.
(185–96)

Where Ovid finds an opportunity for rhetorical 'point', Pope finds
psychological truth. More than this, Eloisa displays intelligence,
self-consciousness and imagination – an imagination in the grip of
those two irresistible agents, passion and memory. She is more
than capable of representing the poet's own concerns in the poem,
and even of (apparently) drawing him into it, by giving him her
commission:

And sure if fate some future Bard shall join
In sad similitude of griefs to mine,
Condemn'd whole years in absence to deplore,
And image charms he must behold no more,
Such if there be, who loves so long, so well;
Let him our sad, our tender story tell;
The well-sung woes will sooth my pensive ghost;
He best can paint 'em, who shall feel 'em most.
(359–66)

Through Eloisa Pope can explore what Ovid merely teases his

heroines with: the passionate desire of suffering to articulate its pain, and find a lenitive in others' understanding; and the creative power of passionate memory, which by describing the outline of a missing presence with feeling and insistence may conjure up the absent lover. Pope had already noted in his juvenile translation of Sappho's letter to Phaon (c.1707) the creative shamelessness of the imagination, which gives back in dreams what it is balked of in reality. He sketches there what later grows into the luxuriant eroticism of Eloisa's dreams, as Sappho (herself a poetess, of course) embraces her imaginary lover with a fervour that is almost satisfaction:

> 'Tis thou art all my Care and my Delight,
> My daily Longing, and my Dream by Night:
> O Night more pleasing than the brightest Day,
> When Fancy gives what Absence takes away,
> And drest in all its visionary Charms,
> Restores my fair Deserter to my Arms!
> Then round your Neck in wanton Wreaths I twine,
> Then you, methinks, as fondly circle mine:
> A thousand tender Words, I hear and speak;
> A thousand melting kisses, give, and take:
> Then fiercer Joys – I blush to mention these,
> Yet while I blush, confess how much they please!
>   (143–54)

In the 'second circle' of Pope's writing, the paradox of 'Fancy giving what Absence takes away' is reconstructed with much greater imaginative investment. In Eloisa's dream, 'Fancy restores what vengeance snatch'd away' with keener delight, and intenser frustration:

> Far other dreams my erring soul employ,
> Far other raptures, of unholy joy:
> When at the close of each sad, sorrowing day,
> Fancy restores what vengeance snatch'd away,
> Then conscience sleeps, and leaving nature free,
> All my loose soul unbounded leaps to thee.
> O curst, dear horrors of all-conscious night!
> How glowing guilt exalts the keen delight!
> Provoking Dæmons all restraint remove,

And stir within me ev'ry source of love.
I hear thee, view thee, gaze o'er all thy charms,
And round thy phantom glue my clasping arms.
I wake – no more I hear, no more I view,
The phantom flies me, as unkind as you,
I call aloud; it hears not what I say;
I stretch my empty arms; it glides away:
To dream once more I close my willing eyes;
Ye soft illusions, dear deceits, arise!

(223–40)

If it is characteristic of poetry to lend body to the invisible, and bring dreams to the brink of reality, then Eloisa is as much a poet as Sappho – or Pope. If we are tempted to read her outpouring as an oblique confession of his own experience, we have good reason. But the stress must go on 'oblique'; for Eloisa is supremely aware that her dreams are only dreams, and tossed between their fleeting pleasure and tormenting inadequacy, she takes refuge at last in artistic perspective. She distances herself from her pain with images of other sufferings, and other lovers, who may one day shed tears upon her marble tomb; and offers her story (in a direct apostrophe very uncharacteristic of Ovid's heroines) to the 'future Bard', who is also condemned 'to image charms he must behold no more'.

The perfect catharsis of her romantic frenzy, Eloisa foresees, will be its metamorphosis into art – the very poem we are reading. And if we say that Pope is deeply invested in her erotic imagination, we must also say that he shares her faith in art; for whatever 'Breathings of the Heart' went into the power of the poetry, it is the *Epistle* that remains, not the passion – as Pope knew it would.

This poem, with the *Essay on Criticism* and the *Rape of the Lock*, stakes out most irresistibly Pope's claim to be a 'new classic'. For in these poems, he not only demonstrates his mastery of versification and form, and his familiarity with tradition, but reaches through to new combinations of the secret powers of poetry. Epic and mock-epic meet in the *Rape of the Lock*, and in *Eloisa to Abelard* the drama of the heroic epistle merges with the pleasures of the *Metamorphoses*, and of Virgil's 'Orpheus and Eurydice' myth.[20] This is how poetry develops and flourishes, when the genres meet and give birth to new combinations – or as Pope describes the process, in less subtle hands than his own,

> How Tragedy and Comedy embrace;
> How Farce and Epic get a jumbled race.
> (*Dunciad* A. I, 67–8)

This is where the truth that 'literature must always resemble other literature more than it resembles anything else' loses its note of hopeless determinism, and 'neo-classicism' earns its right to be called 'new'.

We can see that it did not have to be so from other of the *Works* of 1717. Admiration for the achievements of the past, and a conviction that he can add something of his own, do not make Pope's efforts in the *Messiah*, the *Temple of Fame*, and *Windsor-Forest*, entirely convincing. We recognise his audacity of conception in the attempt to versify *Isaiah* into a 'sacred eclogue', for instance, but the verse itself betrays what was simplistic in the ambition. The note of Augustan 'sublimity' is facile and the periphrases are faintly absurd, beside the potent exaltation of the original. Pope is serious about the literary power of *Isaiah*, and serious about his imitation of Virgil's sacred eclogue (the 'Pollio') – but he is not serious about the miracles attendant on the coming of the Messiah, and his language lives weakly in a vacuum. Compare the original:

> Hear, ye deaf; and look, ye blind, that ye may see . . . Then the eyes of the blind shall be opened, and the ears of the deaf shall be unstopped. Then shall the lame man leap as an hart, and the tongue of the dumb sing. . . . He will swallow up death in victory; and the Lord God will wipe away tears from off all faces.
> (Isaiah 42:18, 35:5–6, 25:8)

> The SAVIOUR comes! by ancient Bards foretold:
> Hear him ye Deaf, and all ye Blind behold!
> He from thick Films shall purge the visual Ray,
> And on the sightless Eye-ball pour the Day.
> 'Tis he th'obstructed Paths of Sound shall clear,
> And bid new Musick charm th'unfolding Ear.
> The Dumb shall sing, the Lame his Crutch foregoe,
> And leap exulting like the bounding Roe.

No sigh, no Murmur the wide World shall hear,
From ev'ry Face he wipes off ev'ry Tear.

$$(37–46)$$

The magnificent asseverations of the prophecy become – mere assertions, and Pope's poem positively skips to its would-be sonorous conclusion:

Thy *Realm* for ever lasts! thy own *Messiah* reigns! (108)

The problem is both one of imagination, and of technique: Pope's imagination has no point of contact with the Old Testament mentality (though he clearly finds it grand and admirable); and his poetic diction is at its weakest when it is uncomplicated by other considerations, and only has a single, prestigious, undivided meaning to assert. We have noted before Pope's readiness to turn any subject upside-down, and approach his meaning by way of all he does not mean. This preserves his diction, however public and formal, in a state of quivering vitality, asserting and subverting a meaning in the same instant. But where the meaning is too sacred to be subverted, or even, in a sense, to be thought about, he is reduced to assertions which have no underpinning. (It is significant that he compensates himself for the strain this forced seriousness sets up with a risqué burlesque of Psalm 1 elsewhere: suppressed thoughts, like all energy, must find an outlet.)[21]

In *The Temple of Fame* Pope makes a lively adaptation of Chaucer's *House of Fame*, defending the prolonged allegory with energy and conviction ('We find an uncommon Charm in Truth, when it is convey'd by this Side-way to our Understanding' [Opening note]). The static pantomime, by which Fame is introduced to her various adherents – scholars, scandalmongers, soldiers and whomever – is not therefore vulnerable to the charge of excessive straightforwardness. It proved so useful to Pope, indeed, that it became the central motif of that masterpiece of obliquity, *Dunciad* Book IV, where the earlier lines came back to Pope with a vengeance (compare Dulness's reception of her worshippers, *Dunc*. B. IV, 71–90):

Around these Wonders as I cast a Look,
The Trumpet sounded, and the Temple shook,
And all the Nations, summon'd at the Call,
From diff'rent Quarters fill the crowded Hall:

Of various Tongues the mingled Sounds were heard;
In various Garbs promiscuous Throngs appear'd;
Thick as the Bees, that with the Spring renew
Their flow'ry Toils, and sip the fragrant Dew,
When the wing'd Colonies first tempt the Sky,
O'er dusky Fields and shaded Waters fly,
Or settling, seize the Sweets the Blossoms yield,
And a low Murmur runs along the Field.
Millions of suppliant Crowds the Shrine attend,
And all Degrees before the Goddess bend.

                                        (276–89)

But, one glance forward to the court of Dulness, and we see how
little Pope has found to add to Chaucer's vision. Fame is not a
goddess about whom he has complex and conflicting thoughts –
nor can he suppose her to be a threat to civilisation. She provides
the occasion for some mild satire, as when his youthful gallants
beg her support for their sexual bragging (a flatter version of the
Rape of the Lock, III, 15–16),

        The Queen assents, the Trumpet rends the Skies,
        And at each Blast a Lady's Honour dies,

                                        (392–3)

but when Pope's own voice breaks into the poem most unmistakably, it is only to utter the earnest hope that his own relation to
fame will be a disinterested one. He admits to being a 'Candidate
for Praise' – but only on the morally proper terms he has enunci-
ated in the volume's preface:

        Nor Fame I slight, nor for her Favours call;
        She comes unlook'd for, if she comes at all:
        But if the Purchase costs so dear a Price,
        As soothing Folly, or exalting Vice:
        Oh! if the Muse must flatter lawless Sway,
        And follow still where Fortune leads the way;
        Or if no Basis bear my rising Name,
        But the fall'n Ruins of Another's Fame:
        Then teach me, Heaven! to scorn the guilty Bays;
        Drive from my Breast that wretched Lust of Praise;
        Unblemish'd let me live, or die unknown,
        Oh grant an honest Fame, or grant me none!

                                        (513–24)

It is an admirable wish, but not one to supply the heat of creative passion that would fuse the poem into a whole – any more than mankind's appetite for Fame is drawn to a significant conclusion. Fame is courted by Virgil on one hand, and fops on the other, and the issue is good or bad, as the case may be.

In *Windsor-Forest*, too, we may say that Pope has assembled his materials, but has not quite written a poem, to judge by his own highest standards. It may be that the kinds of poetry he was trying to unite will naturally pull against one another: pastoral and politics do not stir the same feelings; and it is certainly difficult to bring the poet's mythological vision to bear on the events of the moment. (The Treaty of Utrecht was signed a few weeks after the poem's first appearance, in 1713, and the poem ends with a celebration of the new peace. The original political-pastoral, begun in 1704 and much revised, had told the history of the Forest.)

One of his models was Virgil's *Georgics*, which had also attempted to draw the timelessness of the world of pastoral into the actuality of Roman history. Virgil presses harder on the analogies between the world of nature and of man than in pastoral, and his subject is no longer shepherds but men, who earn their agricultural living in a country recovering from the ravages of a civil war. If they inhabit a moralised countryside (so that, for instance, a hive of bees is a lesson in rigorous centralism and mutual cooperation) it is because the feelings they bring to the simplest acts are so highly charged. They inhabit a fallen universe, to which only the sane regularities of earth, whether resisting or cooperating with man, give dignity.

But Pope, unlike Virgil, has lived through no civil war, and though he can look at Windsor Forest and calculate the human pain that has gone into its making – the village clearances that created it, the kings who exploited it, the patient tilling that made it fruitful – his description remains at the level of tuneful sympathy. When he locates his theme of national war and peace in the mimic warfare of hunting, it is not the town captured by 'Albion' that is real to him, but the dying agony of a single pheasant:

> Short is his Joy! he feels the fiery Wound,
> Flutters in Blood, and panting beats the Ground.
> Ah! what avail his glossie, varying Dyes,
> His Purple Crest, and Scarlet-circled Eyes,
> The vivid Green his shining Plumes unfold;

His painted Wings, and Breast that flames with Gold?

(113–18)

This, says Pope after Virgil, is to 'compare small things with great'; but according to the poetry, which must be the decisive evidence, it is not the death of the pheasant that is small.

Thus, though the poem was vigorously revised across nearly a decade, and Pope did his utmost to unite his praise of country life with his praise of peace, the various parts operate at levels that cannot be reconciled. He even slips into a mode of automatic classicism that he might have laughed at in a contemporary – the Thames turns into a river-god and applauds among other things, the new churches of London, and the plans for a new Palace at Whitehall. It is not these period stratagems we remember, but the lines where Pope manages to infuse description with his deepest sense of the way the world is put together, and he sees that it is good:

> Here Hills and Vales, the Woodland and the Plain,
> Here Earth and Water seem to strive again,
> Not *Chaos*-like together crush'd and bruis'd,
> But as the World, harmoniously confus'd:
> Where Order in Variety we see,
> And where, tho' all things differ, all agree.

(11–16)

The last major experiment Pope attempted in the *Works* of 1717 was an elegy – the *Elegy to the Memory of an Unfortunate Lady*. It is a nice indication of how his poems were born that he wrote it in spite of 'lacking his corpse' (as his Twickenham editor remarks). Pope knew various ladies who had married disastrously, he had abundant sympathy for the female point of view, and he was in a mood to exploit what the age called 'the Pathetick'. We need no other explanation for what might otherwise seem contradictory: that after employing heroic diction subversively in the *Rape of the Lock*, he is able to use it quite straightforwardly here, and to elevate a parallel subject – a girl's betrayal by her lover, and her suicide. But now the language is used to keep us as far away from the world of trivia as possible, and to render the heroine as nobly vague as if she greeted us from the depths of Roman history. In a sense, she does, for the elegy is an imitation of the Roman elegy, though it has no particular model behind it. Pope is discovering the power implicit in a genre, as so often, and exercising a part of his own nature which in other genres has found no release. Though the poem is highly organised in a formal way – it has a theatrical opening, theological queries, a curse, and its own burial rite – the real purpose, no one can doubt, is the generation of an overpowering emotion.

The problem from our point of view is that the emotion is a peculiarly eighteenth-century one, a liquefied pathos, whose value is much less obvious to us than to Pope. But emotions have a traceable history and are generated in a context: and an age that experienced most of its feelings with checks and balances, and monitored itself with steady self-consciousness, seems to have needed at least one emotional outlet that overwhelmed restraint and sought no balance at all. Hence the poem's air of recklessly 'pulling all the stops out': the metaphor is apter than usual, for it is very much as if Pope were playing a resonating organ, and colouring the tone with the stops of wonder, pathos and indignation. The lady has killed herself in the name of feeling (the details of her history are purposely vague) and only the poet's feeling can compensate her. He tenderly accosts her ghost:

> 'Tis she! – but why that bleeding bosom gor'd,
> Why dimly gleams the visionary sword?
> Oh ever beauteous, ever friendly! tell,
> Is it, in heav'n, a crime to love too well?
> To bear too tender, or too firm a heart,
> To act a Lover's or a *Roman*'s part?
> Is there no bright reversion in the sky,
> For those who greatly think, or bravely die?
>
> (3–10)

This imaginative abandon has its erotic undertow – the soft bosom gored with steel is just the kind of contrast the cult of sensibility cherishes – but the elevated language keeps the effect just within bounds, as in the lovely phrase, 'bright reversion' (a highly general, Latinate form of 'heavenly reward'), by which the poet both declares and confines his emotion. Nonetheless, his language is bright with tears, and easily kindles into fervour when he considers the lady's error – simply to have aspired 'Above the vulgar flight of low desire' (l.12). In this mood, Pope can allege with scorn that the alternative is mere hibernation:

> Most souls, 'tis true, but peep out once an age,
> Dull sullen pris'ners in the body's cage:
> Dim lights of life that burn a length of years,
> Useless, unseen, as lamps in sepulchres.
>
> (17–20)

The poem is about the value of risking emotion to the utmost, and the poet leaves us in no doubt that we are implicated, as much as the lady. If we fail to respond, we shall find ourselves classed with the lady's steely-hearted guardian, for whom Pope saves his most splendid disdain:

> Thus, if eternal justice rules the ball,
> Thus shall your wives, and thus your children fall:
> On all the line a sudden vengeance waits,
> And frequent hearses shall besiege your gates.
> There passengers shall stand, and pointing say,
> (While the long fun'rals blacken all the way)
> Lo these were they, whose souls the Furies steel'd,
> And curs'd with hearts unknowing how to yield.
> Thus unlamented pass the proud away,
> The gaze of fools, and pageant of a day!
> So perish all, whose breast ne'er learn'd to glow
> For others' good, or melt at others' woe.
>
> (35–46)

These lines are a pattern for eighteenth-century sensibility: the revulsion from pride, which divides man from his fellows, from obstinacy ('a curse'), and the deliberate cherishing of all outward-going emotion:

> So perish all, whose breast ne'er learn'd to glow
> For others' good, or melt at others' woe.

'Glow' and 'melt' are loaded terms in Pope's vocabulary. They imply a conception of the heart as volcanic lava that we might have thought belonged to the pre-Romantics. But all the elements of the cult of sensibility were present in Pope's own cult of emotion: and this poem came to be used by the next generation as a kind of test for the susceptibility of the feelings. We have the philosopher Hume's account of making the experiment on the famous blind poet, Thomas Blacklock, in 1742; which, if we cannot quite muster the response ourselves, may nontheless tell us how Pope intended the poem to be received:

> I soon found him to possess a very delicate Taste, along with a passionate Love of Learning. . . . I repeated to him Mr. Pope's Elegy to the Memory of an unfortunate Lady, which I happen'd to have by heart: And though I be a very bad Reciter, I saw it affected him extremely. His eyes, indeed, the great Index of the Mind, cou'd express no Passion: but his whole Body was thrown into Agitation: That Poem was equally qualified, to touch the Delicacy of his Taste, and the Tenderness of his Feelings.[22]

It is striking that Hume, notorious across Europe for his religious scepticism, has no doubt to spare for the cult of emotion. Pope (with others) has placed the value of a permeable heart above discussion.

3

Making It New

The richness and audacity of the *Works* of 1717 make it all the more astonishing that for several years Pope's mind had largely been elsewhere, on the most ambitious undertaking he ever undertook – the translation of Homer's *Iliad*. What drew him into it, he later told Spence, 'was purely the want of money';[1] but having once conceived of this vast undertaking, he embarked on it in the most splendid manner, with a contract that marked a watershed in publishing history. Publishing by public subscription was a method which did away with the need for a patron (all the subscribers became patrons of a sort) and also secured the poet's profit in advance, as Dryden had discovered in his handsome subscription volume of Virgil (1697). But Pope's contract with the rival publisher to Dryden's, Lintot, was the basis of a fortune: six volumes for which he earned two hundred guineas each, plus seven hundred and fifty copies of the translation – on the best paper, with choice engravings – to distribute among subscribers to his own profit (£4500 or so). Lintot's share of the bargain was possession of the copyright and the proceeds of publishing the poem in various larger and smaller formats, on cheaper paper.

Homer's *Iliad* and *Odyssey* (Pope later contracted to translate both) were the conspicuous gaps in the library of English versions of the classics that had been built up since 1660. Dryden had translated the first book of the *Iliad* but had not lived to do more; and the reader who wished to reach through to the 'Father of Verse' in English had a choice between a prosy translation from the French,[2] or the rough and comically inadequate poetry of John Ogilby (1660), which revealed and obscured Homer's power in the same moment:

> His Teeth then stern *Achilles* arming gnasht,
> Flame from his burning Eyes, like Lightning, flasht,

Grief gnawes His heart, His bosome swells with Rage,
Preparing 'gainst the *Trojans* to engage.[3]

But if it was clear that a new translation was needed, it was not
clear in all quarters that Pope should be the author of it. Party
feeling animated the public attitude to translators, as to so much
else, and the hope of co-opting such a powerful voice from the
heroic past stirred political rivalry, of just the kind Pope most
wished to avoid. As a result, he had no sooner signed his contract
with Lintot, than a rival 'Whig' translation was in preparation with
the other major publisher of the day, Jacob Tonson. This translation was by a member of Addison's clique and had his powerful
voice in its favour – as well as his hand in the manuscript; though
Addison continued to support Pope's venture in the same breath, a
deviousness for which Pope never forgave him.[4] This translation
sank without trace after the publication of the first book, in the
rising tide of acclaim for Pope's; but while Pope was still collecting
subscriptions for his undertaking, conscious that, if his first
volume failed, subscriptions for the subsequent ones would be
cancelled, it represented a serious threat.

He was also attacked on all the obvious grounds: for being
Catholic, undersized, mercenary and knowing no Greek. This last
charge is still repeated, by those who do not closely consider what
it means to 'know' a language, and suppose that the dictionary is
the final arbiter of sense. A poet's intimacy with the functioning of
his own language gives him an *entrée* into many others, his ear tells
him more, and his eye for the key word is more accurate, than the
ordinary reader's. Beyond this, Pope read his Greek the way every
other educated man of the period did, save the professional
scholars: in a bilingual edition, with the Greek on one page and a
Latin crib on the other – the Latin operating as a translator's
Esperanto that imitated the Greek grammar and compound words,
and enabled the reader to read into the original what he saw must
be there.[5] In addition, Pope sifted all the available translations for
whatever they could supply – notes, formulations, or insight – and
waded through the voluminous commentaries in Greek, Latin and
French that had been accumulating on Homer ever since that of
Eustathius, Bishop of Thessalonica, in the twelfth century. (This
last, particularly copious work he was glad to read in digests
prepared by his friend Parnell, and other scholars.) From these
materials he extracted the annotations on Homer's geography,

history, customs and morals which were an important part of his
offer to the subscribers.[6]

'THAT POETICAL WONDER . . . WHICH NO AGE OR NATION CAN PRETEND TO EQUAL'

This was Johnson's estimate of Pope's translation, and one that
was generally shared, until the great shift of taste that we call
Romanticism. His assumption is that the translation is 'poetical',
and after considering the undertaking in a financial and social
light, it is as poetry we must now consider it. That is certainly how
Pope viewed it himself, in the intervals between his nightmares
(that he would never finish the work) and his sense of oppression
by learned authorities. Were not Homer and he collaborators? As
he describes this new 'siege of Troy' to his Catholic friend Caryll,

> I must confess the Greek fortification does not appear so
> formidable as it did, upon a nearer approach; and I am almost
> apt to flatter myself, that Homer secretly seems inclined to
> correspond with me, in letting me into a good part of his
> designs. There are, indeed, a sort of underling auxiliars to the
> difficulty of the work, called commentators and criticks, who
> would frighten many people by their number and bulk. These lie
> entrenched in the ditches, and are secure only in the dirt they
> have heaped about 'em with great pains in the collecting it. But I
> think we have found a method of coming at the main works by a
> more speedy and gallant way than by mining under ground; that
> is, by using the poetical engines, wings, and flying thither over
> their heads.[7]

The work Pope had done to bring himself into 'secret correspondence' with Homer went back to his childhood: those ramblings in the library which had introduced him to Ogilby's translation at the age of eight, and given him a pleasure so intense he was
still speaking of it 'with a sort of rapture' at the end of his life.[8]
Homer's epics were not a challenge to be met by neat versification
and judicious consultation of the authorities, as they were for
Pope's rival; they were a rooted experience, interconnected and
entwined with all Pope's other reading, and much of his writing
too. As his ramblings took him farther abroad, to Virgil and Ovid,

Tasso and Ariosto, he must have traced what Homer meant to these others as accurately as he registered what Homer meant to his own work – and the stock assumption that Homer was the 'Father of Verse' was no cliché to him.

Literature, as we have so often noted, has a genealogy as traceable as our own. The Greeks themselves said their later tragedies were but 'dishes from the banquet of Homer'; the Romans acknowledged that their literature was essentially the Greek menu, reheated; and all the literatures of Renaissance Europe gloried in their derivation from Roman interpretations of the Greeks. It was Homer who peopled western literature with its stock characters, its eloquent heroes, vulnerable old men, loyal servants, flirts, and faithful or unfaithful wives; and gave it its major themes: the conflict between love and duty, war and peace, innocence and knowledge, meaning and meaninglessness. Even the non-epic genres, like pastoral and satire, could be glimpsed in embryo in Homer, in the pastoral similes for the action, or the railing speech of sardonic Thersites. For a poet to know his Homer as Pope did, it was not a matter of knowing the stories of the epics, but of discovering the original 'matter' of western literature – and of recognising in the same instant how that 'matter' was still embodied in himself, and generating new creations, as a scientist researching DNA would be implicated down to his last fibre in the process he was investigating.

Thus Pope brought to the translating of Homer something more than a scholastic knowledge of Greek: a knowledge of what Homer had meant to the west, and an original poet's intuition of what would have to be done to make that meaning visible to a contemporary audience. These were those 'poetical engines, wings' on which he intended to fly over the heads of the commentators and critics; and the reader who begins to fear that the translation does not sound a very faithful one, might pause to consider for a moment in what fidelity consists. Is it fidelity to the literal words? Homer's words were the product of centuries of the evolution of the oral tradition, drawn from disparate times and places: a composite (as was the 'poet' himself), a language spoken by no one. When a Victorian pedant translated Homer's linguistic quiddities, the effect was risible.[9] Is it fidelity to the metre? Matthew Arnold tried to imitate the Homeric hexameter, and the result was a kind of living fossil, anxiously parading its relation to the original, but impossible to sustain.[10] Is it fidelity to what Homer says? This is surely the nub of the difficulty: for determining what Homer says, and what he means, are processes which naturally flow into one another, and the translator who consciously limits himself to what is 'said' may end up aborting the meaning altogether. The classic 'faithful' translation of our day is that of Richmond Lattimore (Chicago, 1951), but he is no real advance on Ogilby, if we ask ourselves what his translation really means – as here:

> When he saw no sign of his perfect wife within the house,
>   Hektor
> stopped in his way on the threshold and spoke among the
>   handmaidens:
> 'Come then, tell me truthfully as you may, handmaidens:
> where has Andromache of the white arms gone? Is she
> with any of the sisters of her lord or the wives of his brothers?[11]

Lattimore's fidelity really consists of robbing Homer of his coherence, and scrupulously refusing to give him anything in return.

Pope's translation was made at a time when the derivation of the word was still understood. It comes from *trans-ferre*, to 'bring across'; and the assumption of his predecessors, Denham, Cowley and Dryden, was that what chiefly requires to be brought across is the author's greatness – the reason why the translation is being made at all. Hence their insistence on translating poetry into poetry (not the prose or very blank verse of our modern versions), and their determination to make amends to their author, by whatever means available, for what he lost by his passage. 'I have endeavour'd to make *Virgil* speak such *English* as he wou'd himself have spoken, if he had been born in *England*, and in this present Age', says Dryden;[12] and Pope approached Homer in the same radical frame of mind, determined to be faithful to the spirit rather than the letter of his original, and in the midst of all his researches to give pre-eminence to

> that Rapture and Fire, which carries you away with him, with that wonderfull Force, that no man who has a true Poetical spirit is Master of himself, while he reads him. Homer makes you interested and concern'd before you are aware, all at once; whereas Virgill does it by soft degrees. This, I believe, is what a Translator of Homer ought principally to imitate. . . .[13]

Pope could commit himself to Homer's 'Rapture and Fire' because, unlike many translators before and since, he was passionately at one with what he took to be the moral of the poem. Most translations are acts of literary piety towards a heroic, but unmistakably defunct civilisation. But Pope's was the revitalising of a poem he considered to lie at the very foundations of humanism, whose submerged message was a definition of human greatness he shared. We have touched on this in the *Rape of the Lock*, in discussing the speech of Clarissa (modelled on Sarpedon's, *Iliad* XII, 371–96; see above, pp. 45–7). Homer's heroes are no simple-minded war-machines, to risk their lives without asking why; but neither are they intellectuals, to let the moment of action go by in deliberation. They are physically magnificent, and Homer uses animal similes to describe their animal greatness, but their mental greatness is more significant still, and here lies the centre of Pope's interest. Animals too can be brave, and disregard their own pain with perfect singlemindedness when in pursuit of food, territory, or a mate. But it is not given to animals to have visions of how life might be otherwise, and to make their decision to die while possessed of an equal and opposite passion to live. Homer's similes point both the parallel and the distinction, as when Sarpedon is burning to attack the Greek fortification the way a famished lion burns for the sheep in the fold:

> So press'd with Hunger, from the Mountain's Brow
> Descends a Lion on the Flocks below;
> So stalks the lordly Savage o'er the Plain,
> In sullen Majesty, and stern Disdain:
> In vain loud Mastives bay him from afar,
> And Shepherds gaul him with an Iron War;
> Regardless, furious, he pursues his way;
> He foams, he roars, he rends the panting Prey.
>   Resolv'd alike, divine *Sarpedon* glows
> With gen'rous Rage that drives him on the Foes.
> He views the Tow'rs, and meditates their Fall,
> To sure Destruction dooms th'aspiring Wall;
> Then casting on his Friend an ardent Look,
> Fir'd with the Thirst of Glory, thus he spoke.
>   (XII, 357–70)

Sarpedon has a lion's spirit in his breast, and yearns for action as an animal yearns for food. But what inflames him most is the prospect of 'Glory' (the name he will win among men and poets); and his response at the crisis is not to rush forward but to speak – to ask for the explanation an animal does not need. Why is it he risks his life at the forefront of the battle? Because of all the privileges he has received as a chief in peacetime; and because there is no avoiding death in one guise or another. Better to give life away nobly, than have it weakly slip from one's grasp:

> Could all our Care elude the gloomy Grave,
> Which claims no less the fearful than the brave,
> For Lust of Fame I should not vainly dare
> In fighting Fields, nor urge thy Soul to War.
> But since, alas! ignoble Age must come,
> Disease, and Death's inexorable Doom;
> The Life which others pay, let us bestow,
> And give to Fame what we to Nature owe;
> Brave tho' we fall, and honour'd if we live,
> Or let us Glory gain, or Glory give!
>
> (387–96)

The real distinction between men and animals is that for animals, living and dying are ends in themselves, but men must create meaning from life before they assent to it. Since it is evident that life leads directly to the grave, this meaning can only be generated by the way men live, and the terms on which they consent to die: in Sarpedon's case, by living up to his responsibilities as leader, and dying in such a way as to secure immortality in poetry – 'giving to Fame' what he 'owes to Nature'. But what keeps his language free of mere heroics, the 'ours but to do and die' mentality, is his admission that no one would choose to live so expensively if man were not born mortal. The Gods have no such problems in wringing meaning from a brief life. They feast and laugh for eternity, and their appetites are as much an end in themselves as the appetites of animals. It is only man, suspended between the two, who gives away his life for the sake of its meaning.

This world of animal vigour, brief life, and glory, may seem to have few points of contact with the one Pope inhabited. But if we translate the issues into eighteenth-century terms, we may say that every true gentleman would have recognised a version of Sarpe-

don's choice. The obligation to live up to one's responsibilities was
now called Duty, and the keen awareness of the potential cost,
Sensibility: but the resulting compound, a Duty imbued with
feeling, was the supreme aim of Pope's culture. (Hence that
puzzling phenomenon, the androgynous, Grandison-type hero of
the early novel, who combines a feminine quickness of feeling with
masculine audacity.)

There was one other key term Pope thought he had located in
the epic, which mattered to him yet more than these: it was
Reason, that precious faculty so vulnerable to human pride, which
he had placed at the centre of the *Essay on Criticism*:

> Pride, where Wit fails, steps in to our Defence,
> And fills up all the *mighty Void* of *Sense!*
> If once right Reason drives *that Cloud* away,
> *Truth* breaks upon us with *resistless Day*;
> Trust not your self; but your Defects to know,
> Make use of ev'ry *Friend* – and ev'ry *Foe*.
>
> (209–14)

This could serve as an epigraph to the *Iliad*, whose central story,
surprising to those who think of it as a glorification of war, is the
story of the greatest hero's fit of unreason, and his indulgence in a
demonic pride which causes him to withdraw from the fighting.
Achilles has his provocation, for in Book I, Agamemnon robs him
of a slave-girl, a terrible insult in the Mycenaean world; but he
allows his outrage to annihilate all sense of duty, even towards
himself, and sulks in his tent while the Trojans assault the Greeks
with increasing confidence, and Hector kills his dearest friend,
Patroclus, who borrowed Achilles' armour to fight in his place.
When Achilles finally rejoins the battle, it is in a state of rage and
remorse bordering on madness; and he fights now, not as a hero,
but as a butcher, impervious to feeling. He piles Trojan corpses
into the river till he clogs its flow, and having overcome Hector in
their final duel, it is his sadistic pleasure to tell the dying hero that
his body will be left to rot in the air, and be eaten by dogs and
vultures. Then he feeds the revenge that even this cannot satisfy,
by stringing together the corpse at the ankles, and dragging it
round the walls of Troy at the rear of his chariot, in full view of
Hector's tormented parents.

Reverence for a corpse is at the heart of the Homeric code; for the body is the poignant proof that man is not a god, after the spirit, the proof that neither is he an animal, has fled. Even the corpse of an enemy is a sacred object; and in desecrating the body of Hector, Achilles is flouting both heaven and earth, as Homer shows by the speech of Apollo to the other gods in Book XXIV. The god of wisdom denounces Achilles for his lack of *aidos*, human shame, a sense of proper limits – a term Pope translates as Reason, in perhaps his most resonant usage of all:

> Still for one Loss he rages unresign'd,
> Repugnant to the Lot of all Mankind;
> To lose a Friend, a Brother, or a Son,
> Heav'n dooms each Mortal, and its Will is done:
> A while they sorrow, then dismiss their Care;
> Fate gives the Wound, and Man is born to bear.
> But this Insatiate the Commission giv'n
> By Fate, exceeds; and tempts the Wrath of Heav'n:
> Lo how his Rage dishonest drags along
> *Hector*'s dead Earth, insensible of Wrong!
> Brave tho' he be, yet by no Reason aw'd,
> He violates the Laws of Man and God.
>
> (XXIV, 58–69)

The climax of the *Iliad* is not the duel with Hector, but the moment when Achilles accepts this stern rebuke and returns Hector's body to Priam for burial. Enemies as they are, they weep together for 'the Lot of all Mankind': to lose all that they love, and life itself, for that is what being 'mortal' means. And when Achilles submits to the gods, he finally consents to be 'aw'd by Reason' – a 'Reason' conceived as the power which sees humanity's place in the scheme of things, and consents to it in the same moment. Achilles learns to speak like the god of wisdom himself:

> Rise then: Let Reason mitigate our Care:
> To mourn, avails not: Man is born to bear.
> Such is, alas! the Gods severe Decree;
> They, only they are blest, and only free.
>
> (XXIV, 659–62)

It is because Homer's 'war-poem' is organised round the issue, not of human strength, but human reason, that Pope could take

Homer to his heart as a contemporary, and respond to Achilles'
speech without reservation – as we see from his enthusiastic note:

> There is not a more beautiful Passage in the whole *Ilias* than this
> before us: *Homer* to shew that *Achilles* was not a mere Soldier,
> here draws him as a Person of excellent Sense and sound reason:
> *Plato* himself (who condemns this Passage) could not speak more
> like a true Philosopher: And it was a piece of great Judgment
> thus to describe him; for the Reader would have retain'd but a
> very indifferent Opinion of the Hero of a Poem, that had no
> Qualification but mere Strength: It also shews the Art of the Poet
> thus to defer this part of his Character till the very Conclusion of
> the Poem: By these means he fixes an Idea of his Greatness upon
> our Minds, and makes his Hero go off the Stage with Applause.
>   (XXIV, 653n)

THE *ODYSSEY* TRANSLATION, 1725–6

The success of the *Iliad* demanded an answering *Odyssey* translation, to complete the library. But after seven years of wrestling
singlehandedly with the sixteen thousand lines of the *Iliad*, Pope
was in no mood to bind himself over to the same task again (the
Odyssey is not much shorter, at twelve thousand or so). The
method he took was, according to the critics of his own day, sharp
practice, and according to those of ours, 'the least reliable': he
employed two collaborators, Broome and Fenton, who between
them prepared twelve of the twenty-four books of the epic.[14] Pope
then worked over their manuscripts, smoothing out any lapses of
tone and improving the rhythm and diction, and taking over
entirely the management of episodes he considered vital.[15] The
result was a translation best defined as being 'of the School of
Pope', in which the individual hands were not detected by the
subscribers, according to Broome, who commented:

> The most experienced Painters will not wonder at this, who very
> well know, that no Critic can pronounce even of the pieces of
> *Raphael* or *Titian*, which have, or which have not, been worked
> upon by those of their school? when the same Master's hand has
> directed the execution of the whole, reduced it to one character

and colouring, gone over the several parts, and given to each their finishing.

(XXIV, concluding note)

The chief loss was in the architectural coherence of the whole, and the energy of the conception. Sometimes the translation subsides into mere fluency, even in books entirely by Pope: but it is not clear whether that is attributable to his lower level of engagement, or the nature of the *Odyssey* itself (as discussed below).

What made the collaboration into 'a shabby business all round', however (as Mack firmly judges it), was Pope's determination that the subscribers should not know its full extent.[16] He persuaded Broome to admit to only three books of the eight he had contributed, and Fenton, to two of his four, lest all of them should be the losers by the lowering of the translation's prestige. In the event, he was successful, and all of them did well out of the publication: Pope made as much again as he had from the *Iliad*, and Broome and Fenton, £600 and £300 respectively. (Not a scandalous disproportion, since they had not collected the subscriptions from which they were to profit, as Mack explains.) But Pope could not silence the catcalls of Grub Street; and from 1725 to the end of his life, he had to endure the accusation of inventing a new practice:

that of an eminent Poet's taking in *Subscriptions* for any Work, for the sake of *Lucre*, and getting it done by *Hackney-Hands* for the sake of *Idleness*, and at length publishing it under his *own Name*.[17]

There is no clear evidence, however, that Pope's conscience truly pained him, much as he may have deplored the exposure of the subterfuge. We may guess that he reasoned much like the lion in the fable, who goes out hunting with the other animals, but on his own regal terms (as Broome described him to Fenton):[18] that what made the translation valuable was his contribution; that after the work he had done on the manuscripts it was essentially his; and that the subscribers would find the uniformity of the work on reading it, while being told the extent of the collaboration would merely prejudice them against it in advance. His leonine opinion of Broome's pretentions emerges in the later *Dunciad* (although swathed in courteous disclaimers):[19]

Hibernian Politicks, O Swift, thy doom,
And Pope's, translating three whole years with Broome.

(A. III, 327–8)

If we consider the translation as a whole, we may find that the key difference between it and the *Iliad* is not so much the result of the way it was written, as of the way it was conceived. The *Odyssey* is, of course, a very different kind of poem, narrative where the *Iliad* is active, peopled with monsters and low-life characters as well as heroes, and admitting elements of folk-tale and magic. The key-note of the epic is not tragedy but comedy, and any translator must treat it in a different spirit from the *Iliad*. Pope had to search to find a style that was adequate to the high points, yet not too pompous for the narrative, where Homer combines 'Ease and Dignity' in a way very hard to imitate.[20]

But the more radical difficulty, we may guess, lay in the fact that the poem was so accessible. By comparison with the *Iliad*, it seemed almost to translate itself. Instead of having to read and interpret with the utmost energy (Pope found much of the battle-ethos of the *Iliad* appalling, and he was tempted to prefer Sarpedon and Hector to Achilles, on account of their manners),[21] Pope felt a security here that banished all tension – and hence a good deal of effort. The *Odyssey* was, after all, the main source of that poem closer to his civilisation than any, the *Aeneid*, and its hero was not pre-eminent for animal power, rage and (ultimately) submission, but for uninterrupted sanity. Odysseus is human good sense incarnate, and the story of his long and difficult journey home to his faithful Penelope – aided at every point by the goddess of wisdom, Athene – was easily assimilated to the Augustan day-dream of a just and wholly intelligible universe.[22] Thus, Pope's translation radiates conviction, but lacks the inner tension that the strains of the *Iliad* produced. He does not make discoveries here, but celebrates what everyone will recognise as Reason, Truth and Nature.

What gives the *Odyssey* its comparatively comic colouring is that the hero does not weep, like Achilles, for mortality. He prefers it that way; and when the lovely nymph Calypso detains him on her island with the offer of eternal love and immortality, it is his right to live as a human being that he weeps for. He wishes only to return to Penelope, and die in the proper course of things. He is a hero of that Confucian virtue, 'human-heartedness'; and to show his approval, Homer has him shadowed throughout the story by Athene, who looks after him in person or in disguise at every crisis. The immense distance between the gods and man, which gave mortality its dreadful poignancy in the *Iliad* (and which Pope imitated so cleverly in his management of Belinda's sylphs; see p. 43 above), is now mitigated to the point of camaraderie; and the secret of Homer's anthropomorphic religion, that the gods are really human qualities in disguise, is constantly rising into view.[23] Odysseus is not yet the proper eighteenth-century gentleman, as we see when he slaughters Penelope's suitors, then hangs the maids who slept with them; but he makes a very acceptable prototype.

As a result, the places where Pope's translation kindles into life are not so much those where he has built a bridge between his world and Homer's, as those where he finds himself perfectly at home. He delights in such touches as the welcome Odysseus receives from his old dog, Argus, who just has time to wag his tail before he dies (Pope had made a brief version of this as early as 1709, and was passionately considerate of the feelings of all animals)[24] and Odysseus' reunion with Penelope herself is not translated with more sensibility than his meeting with his old father, Laertes. The former king has been reduced to labouring in his own vineyard, and the combination of royalty, degradation, and filial passion, elicits Pope's most Virgilian vein of pathos:

> Beneath a neighb'ring tree, the Chief divine
> Gaz'd o'er his Sire, retracing ev'ry line,
> The ruins of himself! now worn away
> With age, yet still majestic in decay!
> Sudden his eyes releas'd their wat'ry store;
> The much-enduring man could bear no
>   more.
> Doubtful he stood, if instant to embrace
> His aged limbs, to kiss his rev'rend face,
> With eager transport to disclose the whole,
> And pour at once the torrent of his soul?
> Not so: his judgment takes the winding
>   way
> Of question distant, and of soft essay,
> More gentle methods on weak age employs,
> And moves the sorrows to enhance the
>   joys.
> Then to his Sire with beating heart he
>   moves,
> And with a tender pleasantry reproves: . . .

> Great is thy skill, oh father! great thy toil,
> Thy careful hand is stamp'd on all the
>   soil, . . .
> On ev'ry plant and tree thy cares are
>   shown,
> Nothing neglected, but thy self alone.
>   (XXIV, 269–84, 287–8, 292–3)

Homer's Odysseus also weeps at the sight of his father, but the speech he makes is apparently to test him: in a terse, and not wholly intelligible formula, 'he tried him first with mocking words'. To Pope the only explanation possible for the hero's indirection is compassion for frailty, and the eagerness of his own 'beating heart'. Behind this highly-charged scene of filial piety we can glimpse Virgil's Aeneas and Anchises, and the picture of suffering old Priam in the *Iliad* (re-rendered with almost reckless pathos in *Aeneid* II). The vulnerability of old age, its exposure of the gulf between mental dignity and physical indignity, invariably touches Pope as passionately as it does Virgil. In the *Iliad* he lavished some of his best poetry and most heartfelt annotation on Priam and aged Nestor;[25] and here, the moment when Ulysses finally embraces Laertes, is rendered with more natural passion than Penelope herself can stir. All the protective tenderness Pope felt for his own parents, and for fragility in general, pulses through these lines, and multiplies Homer's one kiss by a 'thousand'. Ulysses has made Laertes believe that he is dead, and the old man covers his head with ashes:

> Quick thro' the father's heart these accents ran;
> Grief seiz'd at once, and wrapt up all the man;
> Deep from his soul he sigh'd, and sorrowing spread
> A cloud of ashes on his hoary head.
> Trembling with agonies of strong delight
> Stood the great son, heart-wounded with the sight:
> He ran, he seiz'd him with a strict embrace,
> With thousand kisses wander'd o'er his face,
> I, I am he; oh father rise! behold
> Thy son, with twenty winters now grown old;
> Thy son, so long desir'd, so long detain'd,
> Restor'd, and breathing in his native land . . .
> Smit with the signs which all his doubts explain,

His heart within him melts; his knees sustain
Their feeble weight no more; his arms alone
Support him, round the lov'd *Ulysses* thrown;
He faints, he sinks, with mighty joys opprest:
Ulysses clasps him to his eager breast.

(XXIV, 367–78, 401–6)

Clearly, this emotion is offered for us to share, and consciously to
value ourselves for sharing. Reason, in Pope's emotional organisation, is not at all opposed to Sensibility. Reason tells us to bear – but
humanity tells us to feel; and the man who felt nothing at such a
climax would not be worthy of the name.

We may read the Homer translations with a paradoxical sense
that not only has Pope found in these poems the earliest definition
of human greatness, but also the paradigm of eighteenth-century
emotionalism. The *Iliad* gives less scope for this vein of pathos than
the *Odyssey*, but even here there are moments where we recognise
the author of the *Elegy to the Memory of an Unfortunate Lady*, laying
his curse on insensibility:

So perish all, whose breast ne'er learn'd to glow
For others' good, or melt at others' woe.

At the moment of the reconcilliation between Achilles and Priam,
for instance, Pope works their tears up to flood-level, and makes a
pointed contrast between the courage we expect of a hero, and the
feeling we expect of a man:

Now each by turns indulg'd the Gush of Woe;
And now the mingled Tides together flow:
This low on Earth, that gently bending o'er,
A Father one, and one a Son, deplore:
But great *Achilles* diff'rent Passions rend,
And now his Sire he mourns, and now his Friend.
Th'infectious Softness thro' the Heroes ran;
One universal, solemn Show'r began;
They bore as Heroes, but they felt as Man.

(XXIV, 638–46)

This 'universal, solemn Show'r' is not at all Homeric, but very
much the moral Pope found at the heart of these poems: man's

destiny is a cause for tears (*sunt lachrymae rerum*) and it is because he can weep that he knows himself as man. To all the other long-term influences that stemmed from Pope's translations, we should add that they became one of the patterns by which men of feeling learned how to 'glow' – and when to 'melt'.

4

Rewards of Fame, and its Hazards

THE MOVE TO TWICKENHAM (1718)

When Pope began the *Iliad* translation, he was a rising young poet from a country background, with some famous friends and protectors; when he ended it, he was the country's unofficial laureate, rich, independent, and in a position (as he liked to say) to 'fling off Lords by dozens'. The move away from Binfield in Windsor Forest began in 1716, when Pope and his parents transferred to Chiswick, partly, apparently, to avoid a new tax-burden on their property as Catholics, but also to make it easier for him to conduct his literary affairs in London. It was here that his father died in 1717, and Pope began his long career as his ageing mother's chief support, which lasted with great tenderness on both sides until her death, aged 90 (1733).

In Chiswick Pope was also closer than before to the world of the court, whose summer residence was Hampton Court Palace, and to his increasing number of aristocratic friends: the ladies-in-waiting around Princess Caroline, the Dukes of Shrewsbury and Argyll, the portrait-painter Sir Godfrey Kneller, the benignly rakish Lord Bathurst and, most important, his close neighbour Lord Burlington, the arbiter of architectural taste. On his father's death, Pope invested his new wealth in property, and moved with his mother to a home on the banks of the Thames at Twickenham, still conveniently close to London, but outside the forbidden limits. Here, he was able to indulge his tastes for architecture and gardening at luxurious length, and he improved the nondescript house and a five-acre garden into a miniature 'Palladian' estate, to gladden the heart of Lord Burlington. The house eschewed grandeur for elegance and compactness, and was hung with Pope's large collection of his friends' portraits; and the garden, for all its modest size, was made to incorporate no fewer than three artificial

77

mounts, a wilderness, some sunny glades, woodland, and a bowling green – as well as vegetable beds and hothouses for fruit, the owner's particular pride. Beneath the main road to London, which awkwardly cut off the house from the garden, Pope created his most famous piece of ingenuity, a grotto with a spring running through it, whose waters sparkled in the mirrors placed in the ceiling and in the mineral ores and spars that studded the grotto walls.[1]

Here too he was able to indulge his pleasure in hospitality, and he received his guests with a fine indifference to their current political or social status, offering them the produce of the garden and locality with a pleasant sense of allusion: this was how Horace had lived outside Rome, on his Sabine farm:

> Between Excess and Famine lies a mean,
> Plain, but not sordid, tho' not splendid, clean.
>   (*Imit. Hor. Sat.* II, ii, 47–8)

Twickenham became the source of his values and the exemplification of them, and when he came to imitate Horace's satires in the 1730s, it was Twickenham he praised for the essential Roman virtues:

> Content with little, I can piddle here
> On Broccoli and mutton, round the year;
> But ancient friends, (tho' poor, or out of play)
> That touch my Bell, I cannot turn away.
> 'Tis true, no Turbots dignify my boards,
> But gudgeons, flounders, what my Thames affords.
> To Hounslow-heath I point, and Bansted-down,
> Thence comes your mutton, and these chicks my
>   own:
> From yon old wallnut-tree a show'r shall fall;
> And grapes, long-lingring on my only wall,
> And figs, from standard and Espalier join:
> The dev'l is in you if you cannot dine. . . .
> My lands are sold, my Father's house is gone;
> I'll hire another's, is not that my own,
> And yours my friends? thro' whose free-opening gate
> None comes too early, none departs too late;
> (For I, who hold sage Homer's rule the best,

Welcome the coming, speed the going guest.)
(ibid., 137–48, 155–60)[2]

This poetical, considered, and delightfully comfortable retreat
was Pope's chief reward for the previous decade's labours; and it
became his safest retreat from the consequences of those of the
following decade, rising to the supreme discomfort embodied in
the *Dunciad* (1728). The price of his fame was exposure to detrac-
tion and defamation, and his eminence acted as a goad to pam-
phleteers, who did not fail to take the various openings offered
them, by the *Odyssey* collaboration, by Pope's edition of
Shakespeare (1725), and his mock-treatise on rhetoric, *Peri Bathous:
or, Martinus Scriblerus, His Treatise of the Art of Sinking in Poetry*
(1728). Pope became the target of so much abuse that he was able
to collect the offending pamphlets in six privately-bound volumes
for ready reference and quotation in his own satires; while his
Grub Street enemies tasted the bile they could not digest for the
rest of his career. As the annalist of Pope's war with the Dunces
phrases their bewilderment:

Who was this Alexander Pope anyway? The son of a farmer or a
hatter at best, they said, in an attempt to cut this man down
socially. What right had he to a villa at Twickenham, to a
comfortable income, and visiting acquaintance with half the
peerage? Why should he be accepted on equal terms in house-
holds where their own acquaintance was among the footmen –
and he a Catholic, a Jacobite, legally a pariah, to boot? Furth-
ermore, he had not sold himself to a political party or toadied a
patron. Instead, he had beaten the booksellers at their own
game. This was what really hurt. That Pope had done it proved
that it could be done; the fact that they could not do it too, and
knew it, was an ever-present reminder that what he said about
them was true: they *had* missed their calling; if a man had the wit
and inventiveness, the public to support him was already there.
All Pope had had to do was publish an expensive translation of
Homer, the proceeds going mostly to himself. And this when he
did not even know Greek![3]

POPE AS EDITOR

Pope had made his name a valuable commodity, and booksellers were ardent to exploit it to their joint advantage – just as Pope's literary friends were interested in exploiting his taste and judgement in the presentation of their works. Hence we find him, after the *Iliad* translation, acting for some years more as an editor than a poet. He prepared his dead friend Parnell's poems for the press (1721) and revised the papers and poems of the Duke of Buckinghamshire, in two volumes (1723); he accepted the editorship of a prestigious new Shakespeare in six volumes (only the second annotated edition that had been made), which appeared in 1725, and at the same time 'edited' the translations of Broome and Fenton for their joint *Odyssey*.

Biographers have speculated on what kind of crisis might underlie this long lapse of creativity, which they date from the beginning of the *Iliad* translation; but it is very doubtful whether Pope himself considered it a lapse, and perhaps only a post-Romantic generation would raise such a question. We readily assume that the creative artist revolts from the kind of work that translating and editing involve: but as we have seen, Pope's concept of translation was highly active and creative, and the role of editor he seems to have viewed as continuous with that of artist, not as antagonistic. Where another mind might lurch from one realm to the other with pain, Pope's moves elegantly to and fro; and the poet who gave us the *Works* of 1717 is also the editor who later supplies the sources and notes at the foot of the page. This does not mean that he cannot be obsessed by creation in the proper Romantic mode – as he launched into the *Iliad* he said, 'I scarce see what passes under my nose, and hear nothing that is said about me. To follow Poetry as one ought, one must forget father and mother, and cleave to it alone'[4] – but beside this we need to set another picture, that of an editor frowning over a text, and darting his quill at the margin in a different dream of concentration.

With Pope's passion for correctness, it was, he said, 'as pleasant to [him] to correct as to write';[5] and with his sense of responsibility towards civilisation at large, amending and annotating other men's works was not unlike improving his own. We can see from the books in his library that he did this as a matter of course, as a gardener habitually stoops to pull up weeds in other men's gardens;[6] and when we consider how far his original works were (in the widest, neo-classic sense) also translations, it is easier to see how editorial hack-work and creativity were not painfully opposed for Pope. Amending a text to make it more intelligible was one step on the road to helping the reader understand it; writing annotations on its beauties was a second; and translating it in such a way that its best qualities became evident – or recreating it entirely – was a continuation of the same process.

Nonetheless, we may still be startled at times by what Pope defined as 'correctness'. We should expect him to be severe upon weak versification, tautology, or lapses of tone; but we might not be prepared for the fierce literal-mindedness that led him to strike out of his own pastoral *Summer*, the couplet

> Your praise the tuneful birds to heav'n shall bear,
> And list'ning wolves grow milder as they hear,
> (79–80)

on the grounds that there were no wolves in England; or to comment on a rival's pastorals, with withering sarcasm,

> Mr. *Philips*, by a Poetical Creation, hath raised up finer Beds of Flowers than the most industrious Gardiner; his Roses, Lillies and Daffadils blow in the same Season.[7]

But for Pope, poetry had by no means severed its ties with Truth and Reason. One of his many quarrels with the Dunces was that their verse so wantonly did. He belonged to a different school, which submitted, almost grimly, to the logic of the external world; perhaps for the very reason that the 'wings' of poetry so easily rapted the poet out of it. Pope cherished the facts of nature, as he cherished the rules of grammar and logic, as miniature forms of the tonic resistance set up by the world to the imagination; and it was no trivial error, to his way of thinking, to make 'Roses, Lillies and Daffadils blow in the same Season.' The mind that could so override the facts of botany would hardly be restrained by anything else. Poetry like this does not transcend reality – it merely casts it aside, without examining it.

But if Pope's passion for good sense in poetry was part of his strength, it had peculiar consequences when applied to a poet who was aiming at something quite different. As an editor of Shakespeare, Pope was somewhat in the position of a gardener from Kew put down in the tropics – awestruck, but busy. Since Shakespeare was the greatest of dramatists, he should appear so, and Pope set about adjusting the text in both minor ways (regularising the scansion, improving the punctuation, and dividing the scenes) and major ones (degrading substandard lines or speeches to the bottom of the page, and resolving textual difficulties). Much of this labour was unavoidable, given the rough state of the early printing, and modern editors have done the same; but we catch the vast distinction between an age of linguistic buccaneering like Shakespeare's, and an age of linguistic decorum, in Pope's reluctance to let Macbeth say that his bloody hand would 'the multitudinous seas incarnadine', or mad Lear cry out at the sight of Gloucester, 'Hah! Goneril, with a white beard!'. (Pope adopts the flat quarto reading, 'Hah! *Gonerill!* hah *Regan!*'.) Dignity in language and station fetter Pope's imagination as they never fettered Shakespeare's, and thus we lose such vigorous touches as the remark, of the newly-contrite King Lear, 'a sovereign shame so elbows him' (Pope, 'so bows him'), or Hamlet's self-excoriation, 'Yet I,/A dull and muddy-mettled rascal, peak/Like John-a-dreams, unpregnant of my cause,/And can say nothing' – which Pope delicately relegates to the bottom of the page; just as he adjusts 'grunt' to 'groan' in 'who would fardels bear,/To grunt and sweat under a weary life.' There were words in the eighteenth century unpoetical to the point of comedy, and 'grunt' was one of them.

Pope's method of 'improving' Shakespeare into neo-classic decorum was as far as possible from present-day editorial principles. It was an artist's response, not a scholar's, and it left him correspondingly vulnerable to attack from those who, without being philologists in the modern sense, were beginning to see that Elizabethan usages had a validity of their own. Lewis Theobald, scholar and hack playwright, followed up Pope's edition with a volume triumphantly exposing 'the many errors, as well committed, as unamended, by Mr. Pope', *Shakespeare Restored* (1726). He gloried in his fidelity to Shakespeare's text, and since some of Theobald's emendations have persisted to our day, it is common to view his labours with respect; but a glance at the volume shows that, when Pope responded by deriding Theobald in the *Dunciad*, his repulsion stemmed from more than hurt pride: he was fighting to maintain the connection between editorial labour and creativity that he felt in himself, and which Theobald rudely ruptures.

Theobald's decisions, whether right or wrong, are announced

with the same immovable conceit, and a blank disregard for the art he is supposed to be serving. Of his first four points scored against Pope's *Hamlet*, two are about commas, and one creates a line that is an offence to the ear ('Had made his course t'illum*ine* that part of heaven', I.1.40, for 'illume'). The same mind that sensibly restores 'His canon 'gainst self-slaughter' (Pope, 'Cannon') quite pointlessly proposes 'horribly' for 'horridly' ('So horridly to shake our disposition', I.4.55) and supports it with sixteen illustrations, and the boast, 'I could have amass'd twenty times as many.' Theobald properly defends Shakespeare's practice of making verbs out of nouns ('. . . power/To business with the king', I.2.36–7) but not without giving eighteen illustrations more, and seven of adjectives similarly applied. In all this there is a kind of violence of humility towards the text, and a wilful abnegation of judgement (Theobald replaces whatever is prolix and verbose, as I.4.17–38), which sit oddly indeed on the work of the writer who never blotted a line.[8] If Shakespeare is not an artist of Pope's kind, still less is he a pedant of Lewis Theobald's. Though a text prepared on these principles comes closer to authenticity, the message it really conveys is the excitement of the editor, as he struggles with miniature difficulties and ignores anything larger than himself: the tone, spirit and coherence of the works he is serving. He is as happy as an ant on a dung-hill – where he expects us to join him.

POPE AND SWIFT AS COLLABORATORS, 1726–8

If we want to sharpen our impression of what is lost when learning becomes a cover for egotism and aggression, it is instructive to immerse ourselves briefly in the atmosphere of the friendship between Pope and Swift, with all the mutual support and cross-fertilisation it brought with it. In a year of repeated discomforts (1726 saw not only *Shakespeare Restored*, and cries of chicanery about the *Odyssey* collaboration, but the pirate publication of Pope's uncensored letters to Henry Cromwell by Curll – not to mention a severe carriage accident in which Pope nearly drowned), the one unmitigated good was a five-month visit to London of Jonathan Swift.

Pope's friendship with Swift was probably the deepest and most sustaining literary friendship of his life. Other Scriblerians with whom he collaborated in various games and parodies might be easier company, like the wholly benevolent Dr Arbuthnot, or the plump and cheerful Gay, but no other friend's creative imagination seems to have lain so open to Pope as Swift's, and to have invited collaboration so naturally. Their mutual reliance, human and professional, glows through the letters of this period. When Pope was prevented by illness from attending Swift's farewell dinner, Swift wrote (with the gruffness that disguised all his powerful affections),

> My Lord Peterborow spoiled every body's dinner, but especially mine, with telling us that you were detained by sickness. Pray let me have three lines under any hand or pothook that will give me a better account of your health; which concerns me more than others, because I love and esteem you for reasons that most others have little to do with, and would be the same although you had never touched a pen, further than with writing to me.[9]

For his part, Pope felt his loss after such a long visit as an amputation:

> Many a short sigh you cost me the day I left you, and many more you will cost me, till the day you return. I really walk'd about like a man banish'd, and when I came home, found it no home. 'Tis a sensation like that of a limb lopp'd off, one is trying every minute unawares to use it, and finds it is not. I may say you have used me more cruelly than you have done any other man; you have made it more impossible for me to live at ease without you: Habitude itself would have done that, if I had less friendship in my nature than I have.[10]

There is, of course, an element of parade in such letters: the authors are conscious of how highly their friendship becomes them (and in Pope's case, how well it would look in print); but that is not incompatible with a sense of profound gratitude, for having a friend who can elicit such feelings and liberate them from the constraints imposed by life elsewhere. (Among Swift's current irritations were his failure to move Walpole's consideration for neglected Ireland, and confirmation that his exile was permanent, unless he changed his politics.) When they loudly value each other, it is to celebrate something worth the celebration; and that it was no mere matter of words, we know from the creativity they released in one another, particularly Pope's responsiveness to Swift.

One major result of Swift's visit was their agreement to collaborate on a series of *Miscellanies*, where their lighter pieces, in prose as well as verse (legal spoofs, maxims, mock-treatises, Scribleriana generally), would find a home; and four such volumes appeared (1727–32). The exhilarating freedom they found in shared ventures and intellectual sympathy, shows in such delightful responses as Pope's to *Gulliver's Travels*, published as Swift returned to Ireland. Pope could not resist supplying Lilliput with a Poet Laureate, Titty Tit, Esq., and the 'Man-Mountain' with *A Lilliputian Ode*:

> In Amaze
> Lost, I gaze!
> Can our Eyes
> Reach thy Size?
> May my Lays
> Swell with Praise
> Worthy thee!
> Worthy me!
> Muse inspire,
> All thy Fire!
> Bards of old
> Of him told,
> When they said
> *Atlas* Head
> Propt the Skies:
> See! and believe your Eyes!
> (1–16)

The Laureate exclaims for several more verses – but equally unexpected is the opportunity to eavesdrop on the *Lamentation of Glumdalclitch, for the Loss of Grildrig* (Gulliver) in Brobdignag. All Pope's expertise with sylphs and gnomes, and mastery of the Ovidian heroine's prattling pathos, mingle with the clues in the original:

> "Dost thou bewilder'd wander all alone,
> "In the green Thicket of a Mossy Stone,
> "Or tumbled from the Toadstool's slipp'ry Round,

"Perhaps all maim'd, lie grov'ling on the Ground?
"Dost thou, inbosom'd in the lovely Rose,
"Or sunk within the Peach's Down, repose?
"Within the King-Cup if thy Limbs are spread,
"Or in the golden Cowslip's Velvet Head;
"O show me, *Flora*, 'midst those Sweets, the Flow'r
"Where sleeps my *Grildrig* in his fragrant Bow'r!
   "But ah! I fear thy little Fancy roves
"On little Females, and on little Loves;
"Thy Pigmy Children, and thy tiny Spouse,
"The Baby Play-things that adorn thy House,
"Doors, Windows, Chimnies, and the spacious Rooms,
"Equal in Size to Cells of Honeycombs.
"Hast thou for these now ventur'd from the Shore,
"Thy Bark a Bean-shell, and a Straw thy Oar? . . ."
   She said, but broken Accents stopt her Voice,
Soft as the Speaking Trumpet's mellow Noise:
She sobb'd a Storm, and wip'd her flowing Eyes,
Which seem'd like two broad Suns in misty Skies. . . .

                                            (41–58, 71–4)

The King of Brobdingnag also gains a philosophical speech on the miniature Gulliver, and the horses of England address Gulliver on their enslavement, but the nicest literary joke is Mary Gulliver's reproach to her alienated husband, in the tones of Eloisa:

> My Bed, (the Scene of all our former Joys,
> Witness two lovely Girls, two lovely Boys)
> Alone I press; in Dreams I call my Dear,
> I stretch my Hand, no *Gulliver* is there!
> I wake, I rise, and shiv'ring with the Frost,
> Search all the House; my *Gulliver* is lost!
> Forth in the Street I rush with frantick Cries:
> The Windows open; all the Neighbours rise:
> *Where sleeps my* Gulliver? *O tell me where?*
> The Neighbours answer, *With the Sorrel*
> *Mare*.
>
>   (39–48)

These poems were prefixed to later editions of *Gulliver's Travels* itself, and perhaps there could be no happier demonstration of what friendship meant to Pope and Swift: liberty to frolic within the precinct of another's genius, and to bring one's own best powers to bear, with a tribute of admiration that is also pure fun. The two artists meet in such trifles like two performers on the high trapeze, imitating free flight through the strictest discipline of muscle and timing.

If we are to believe a footnote of Pope's, he also had a more specific reason to be grateful for Swift's companionship in 1726. He credits Swift with snatching from the fire the first sketch of what became the *Dunciad*, and persuading him to proceed with it.[11] 'It was my principal aim in the entire work to perpetuate the friendship between us', he assures Swift in 1729,[12] and the opening invocation is a magnificent tribute to him as satirist, pamphleteer, and protector of Ireland:

> O thou! whatever Title please thine ear,
> Dean, Drapier, Bickerstaff, or Gulliver!
> Whether thou chuse Cervantes' serious air,
> Or laugh and shake in Rab'lais' easy Chair,
> Or praise the Court, or magnify Mankind,
> Or thy griev'd Country's copper chains unbind;
> From thy Bæotia tho' Her Pow'r retires,
> Grieve not at ought our sister realm acquires:
> Here pleas'd behold her mighty wings out-spread,
> To hatch a new Saturnian age of Lead.
>
> (A. I, 17–26)

THE DUNCIAD, 1728

The glimpse inside the mind of Theobald afforded by his book, proved all that was needed to elicit from Pope's imagination a vision that had been developing there since his early satire on Settle:

> Begone ye Criticks, and restrain your Spite,
> *Codrus* writes on, and will for ever write . . .

Why was the flow of bad writing so unquenchable? Because it was so much easier to write badly than well. But why did the Theobalds of this world not try harder? Because they were in love with their own productions, and refused to acknowledge any talent larger than their own. And how did they justify themselves? They were under the sure protection of a goddess and did not need to – the Goddess Dulness, defender of mental laxity in all times and places.

Pope brought together under the heading of Dulness activities we would normally think of as distinct: the editor's refusal to consider the wider meaning of his text, the writing of a bad translation, or the production of a catchpenny pantomime. Theobald had, like many other hack writers, turned his hand to all three; but what brought them all together in Pope's mind was the underlying spirit of irresponsibility. If bad art, as we noted above, 'is a kind of crime, akin to poisoning the public wells' and the bad artist 'can make us less than we might have been, or can undo what we were', then every word Theobald wrote was helping to undo Pope's work. No matter whether his plays were incoherent to the point of hilarity – like *The Persian Princess, or, The Royal Villain* (1715):

> (MEMNON, to Mirvan and the High Priest of the Sun:)
> By Heav'n! it fires my frozen Blood with Rage,
> And makes it scald this aged Trunk, to think
> Our *Persia*, that for Discipline and Rule
> Stood Candidate with *Sparta*, rough in War,
> Patient of Labour, and disdaining Ease,
> Should now, debas'd into licentious Riots,
> Make Appetite her God: – and scorn to bow
> Before the Rising Sun, whilst Midnight Lamps
> Attend her Sports beyond the setting Stars –[13]

even this compound of mixed metaphor, cliché and moralistic posture carried with it a message from the great goddess Dulness: that when we do not wish to think, the language will think for us, and when we do not wish to be moral, we can ape the moral attitudes of the dead past. It is no accident that this play required a bawdy Epilogue to wake the audience out of its torpor, and that it took the form of an innuendo that had cobwebs on it in Charles II's time – that the playgoers are tingling for more urgent, and probably risky, pleasures:

> Lord! on what Thorns you sit, and seem so nettled,

Because kind Madam yields, and Bargain's settled.
For Heav'n's Sake, been't thus eager for the Lure,
You may too soon repent the hot Amour.
Better be teiz'd with ten dull *Poetasters*,
Than single *Recipe* – for Love's Disasters!
One Hearty Curse, and *Epilogue's* forgot:
But when that other Malady's your Lot,
You will not only Curse, but – curse, and *rot*.[14]

Pope looked deep into this mind that was dull even when lewd, and vacuous even when annotating Shakespeare, with not only horror but fascination. What a power she was, this goddess! – as all-embracing as mist, as seductive as deep sleep. Nor was Theobald her only votary, or Dulness the only name she had gone under in poetry: Pope recognised her in Ovid's Somnus (Sleep), Boileau's La Mollesse (Laxity, the spirit of the unreformed Church in *Le Lutrin*), and the midwife who had given birth to Dryden's Og (Shadwell):

> The Midwife laid her hand on his Thick Skull,
> With this Prophetick blessing: *Be thou Dull*;
> Drink, Swear and Roar, forbear no lew'd delight,
> Fit for thy Bulk, doe anything but write.[15]

She was to be found everywhere, in short, that men yearned to be spared the burden of their humanity, and all it entailed: thought, alertness, effort. She was the presiding spirit of the end of civilisation.

With the experience of Homer behind him, and of Homer's definition of how man differs from the animals, Pope found the idea of an anti-epic, a *Dunciad*, irresistible. We have already noted how he delighted in approaching a subject back-to-front, and conjuring qualities out of negatives. But in deciding to construct a whole poem in praise of Dulness, he was preparing to indulge his vein of paradox to the limit. Just as the *Rape of the Lock* defies us to say whether love or mockery predominates, so an epic celebration of mental fog leaves us stranded between conflicting perceptions: yes, mental relaxation is a wonderful relief – no, it is a treacherous surrender of the powers that make us human. Since epic poetry is about human effort, there could be no more exquisite subversion of it than to apply the epic manner to the numbed failure of effort;

and since Virgil's *Aeneid*, in particular, is about the terrible cost of
founding an empire, no model could be better suited to a satire on
the widening 'empire' of Dulness in the human brain – founded at
no cost at all. Turning Dulness into a goddess has the effect of
magnifying the problem and making it palpable, just as the sylphs
and gnomes magnified the meaning of Belinda's honour. Everything Pope tells us about her, he is really telling us about the
human psyche, and the size of her empire is a way of talking about
the scale of the problem, which implicates everyone who has ever
yawned.[16]

The reader who has no trouble in following Pope thus far, may
nonetheless be puzzled why he insists that the end of civilisation
begins with – bad writing. His epic is dominated by a mock-
Miltonic vision of the cosmic anarchy over which Dulness pres-
ides. (She is 'Daughter of Chaos and eternal Night', see *Paradise
Lost*, II, 890–97.) This anarchy is a literary anarchy, best understood
as a glimpse inside Theobald's brain:

> Here she beholds the Chaos dark and deep,
> Where nameless somethings in their causes sleep,
> 'Till genial Jacob, or a warm Third-day
> Call forth each mass, a poem or a play.
> How Hints, like spawn, scarce quick in embryo lie,
> How new-born Nonsense first is taught to cry,
> Maggots half-form'd, in rhyme exactly meet,
> And learn to crawl upon poetic feet.
> Here one poor Word a hundred clenches makes,
> And ductile dulness new meanders takes;
> There motley Images her fancy strike,
> Figures ill-pair'd, and Similes unlike.
> She sees a Mob of Metaphors advance,
> Pleas'd with the madness of the mazy dance:
> How Tragedy and Comedy embrace;
> How Farce and Epic get a jumbled race;
> How Time itself stands still at her command,
> Realms shift their place, and Ocean turns to land.
> Here gay Description Ægypt glads with showers;
> Or gives to Zembla fruits, to Barca flowers;
> Glitt'ring with ice here hoary hills are seen,
> There painted vallies of eternal green,
> On cold December fragrant chaplets blow,

And heavy harvests nod beneath the snow.
   All these and more, the cloud-compelling Queen
Beholds thro' fogs that magnify the scene:
She, tinsel'd o'er in robes of varying hues,
With self-applause her wild creation views,
Sees momentary monsters rise and fall,
And with her own fool's colours gilds them all.
                                                   (A. I, 53–82)

Pope, no less than the Romantics, believed that the mind is its own world, and its acts of creation are touched with divinity. But it does not therefore follow that what it creates is perfect. The Creation originally depended on discrimination, distinctness, decision ('God said, Let there be light . . . and [He] made two great lights . . . to rule over the day and over the night, and to divide the light from the darkness: and God saw that it was good.' Genesis 1). But the Creation of Dulness is indecisive, involuntary, inane: 'nameless somethings' sleep until kindled into low-grade life by 'genial Jacob', the publisher Jacob Tonson, 'or a warm Third-day' – when the theatre-takings were given to the author. It is the faint hope of gain that turns weak 'Hints', scarcely as alive as frogspawn, into the 'mass' of a poem or play; or perhaps they take the form of 'Maggots', learning to crawl upon 'poetic feet'. (Pope is punning delightfully on the other meanings of 'feet' (metre) and 'maggot' (a perverse idea).) The energy of these acts of creation is not calm and majestic, but frenziedly busy: this is less birth than proliferation, in the style of bacteria. When a mind like Theobald's generates metaphors, they arrive in 'Mobs', and as the 'mazy dance' heats up, the literary genres begin their own orgy in the corner, producing a 'jumbled race' by miscegenation, like Theobald's own pantomimes. The same kind of mind that overrode the facts of botany ('his Roses, Lillies and Daffadils blow in the same Season') here plays havoc with time, space and geography, for its own ease ('How Time himself stands still at her command,/Realms shift their place, and Ocean turns to land'). It is a vast, primal egotism at work, as funny, and as terrible, as an infant's. And in the manner of infantilism, the dull mind is enchanted at its works, precisely because they are its own: Dulness 'with self-applause her wild creation views', and mistakes its grandeur of scale, because she views it through a magnifying fog.
   Pope here is giving us an insight into how Dulness returns the

world to its first chaos. If it is true that 'In the beginning was the Word' – the word being the medium in which man knows himself as man, and the world for what it is – it is equally true that the reduction of the word to meaninglessness is the end of the world as we know it: as Pope sees the final cataclysm,

> She comes! the Cloud-compelling Pow'r, behold!
> With Night Primæval, and with Chaos old.
> Lo! the great Anarch's ancient reign restor'd,
> Light dies before her uncreating word. . . .
>
> (A. III, 337–40)

To give resonace and scale to the ultimate catastrophe requires a cast of thousands, and hence the multitudinous forgotten writers who crowd the epic. Theobald is foremost, as the hero Dulness has chosen to found her empire, but surrounding him are all those whose activities extend her yawn: heavy editors of heavier texts, writers of farces, scribblers of epigrams, pornographic booksellers, fake biographers, theatre impresarios, journalists, ghost-writers, and pedants, all 'nameless names' of whom Pope mock-tenderly but truthfully remarks, 'It is only in this monument that they must expect to survive'.[17] The effect is something like that of Dante's *Inferno*, at once astonishingly detailed, and dreadfully simple; as with Dante, we marvel at the pertinacity that distinguishes sinner from sinner, and the unremitting seriousness that never loses sight of the underlying unity – damnation. (As with Dante, too, the time-scale is comprehensive: more than half the characters Pope names are not his contemporaries.)[18]

What makes it all possible is Pope's editorial passion. From his collection of scurrilous pamphlets against himself, and Grub Street ephemera of every kind, he selects the apposite quotation, or the dreadful blunder, which justifies the inclusion of each name. (The 1728 edition, with initials but no names, was swiftly followed by a fully annotated one, complete with appendices and a bibliography of the Dunces' previous attacks on Pope, in 1729.) Having done painful justice to each individual, and carefully distinguished the vapid from the wilful, and the silly from the sly, he then goes on to expose what the Dunces have in common: their love of meaningless noise, their dirty-mindedness, and their passionate frivolity. Dulness is made to celebrate her coronation of Theobald by staging heroic games, parallel to those in the *Iliad* and *Aeneid*: but now the games involve chasing a ghost-author who vanishes into air, pissing, tickling, and diving with alacrity into the filth at the bottom of a tributary of the Thames.

Pope's conviction that the art of editing is continuous with that of poetry is never better justified than when the editorial apparatus of proper names, and authentic quotations, passes imperceptibly into a mythic vision of what those names signify. He expresses his charge that the Dunces prefer noise to meaning, as a playful challenge from Dulness to make as much racket as possible:

> Now thousand tongues are heard in one loud din:
> The Monkey-mimicks rush discordant in.
> 'Twas chatt'ring, grinning, mouthing, jabb'ring all,
> And Noise, and Norton, Brangling, and Breval,
> Dennis and Dissonance; and captious Art,
> And Snip-snap short, and Interruption smart.
> 'Hold (cry'd the Queen) A Catcall each shall win,
> Equal your merits! equal is your din!'
>
> (A. II, 227–34)

The poetry creates a force-field in which the genuine names of authors collapse into jangling: Pope makes us hear 'Norton' as an illustration of 'Noise', and wonder if 'Brangling' is a name like 'Breval' (it is a variant of 'wrangling'). In 'Dennis and Dissonance' the assonance is so exquisitely flawed that we hear one as an instance of the other; though Dennis's name was no joke to Dennis, and would seem unremarkable in any other context. Under Pope's mythologising gaze the Dunces 'endure a type of historical death and imaginative transfiguration', as Aubrey Williams has it,[19] and the process is central to the poetry – though, of course, it struck the Dunces as supreme effrontery, and caused them to 'besiege' the bookseller on the poem's appearance, with 'Entreaties, Advices, Threats of Law, and Battery, nay Cries of Treason',[20] for to each indignant, wounded ego, the discovery that his actuality had been submerged in his mythological significance was the unkindest cut of all.

It is a fascinating insight into Pope's view of the mutual relations of life and art, that his editorial role went beyond merely collating the materials on which the poem was founded, into actually calling them into existence. It was his own mock-treatise *The Art of Sinking in Poetry* (published two months earlier) that drew on him much of the abuse he repays in the *Dunciad*. This had taken a provocatively zoological approach to authors, and supplied suggestive initials in each category:

4. The *Parrots* are they that repeat *another's* words, in such a hoarse odd voice, as makes them seem their *own*. W.B. W.S. C.C. The Reverend D.D. . . .
8. The *Eels* are obscure authors, that wrap themselves up in their own mud, but are mighty nimble and pert. L.W. L.T. P.M. General C.
9. The *Tortoises* are slow and chill, and, like pastoral writers, delight much in gardens: they have for the most part a fine embroider'd Shell, and underneath it, a heavy lump. A.P. W.B. L.E. The Right Hon. E. of S.[21]

Pope's pleasure in 'milking' the Dunces also shows in the use made in the footnotes of 1729 of their scurrilities of 1728. But lest we begin to feel protective towards the Dunces, at the mercy of a poet with such dangerous powers, we should remember Pope's remark about 'the constant and eternal aversion of all bad writers to a good one'[22] and ask where the provocation began. The Dunces, after all, did not have to write – there were other ways of earning a living; but having committed themselves to the pen, their chief quarrel with Pope was his creative energy and their own impotence, which they exposed even as they denied it. One of the many anonymous pamphlets written in reply to the *Dunciad*, for instance, had for its frontispiece an engraving of Pope as a hunchbacked monkey, inscribed,

> Chuse for this Work a Stump of crooked Thorn,
> Or Log of Poison Tree, from *India* born:
> There carve a *Pert*, but yet a *Rueful* Face,
> Half Man, half Monkey, own'd by neither Race.
> Be his Crown Picked, to One Side reclin'd,
> Be to his Neck his Buttocks closely join'd;
> With Breast protuberant, and Belly thin,
> Bones all distorted, and a shrivell'd Skin.
>   This his Misshapen Form: but say, what Art
> Can frame the monst'rous Image of his Heart.
> Comps'd of *Malice, Envy, Discontent,*
> Like his Limbs crooked, like them impotent.[23]

The violent disregard of the decencies of either life or art in such responses, and the underlying passion to degrade what the author cannot understand, help explain why Pope supplied in the *Dunciad* scenes in which the Dunces' natural habitat is sewage. It is not so much the general accusation of dirty-mindedness he is making, as the comfort he sees them finding in degradation. If there is no such thing as excellence, their mental torpor is justified; so long as no one writes better than they do, there can be no competition. The idea that writers such as these compete only to reach the bottom first, has been growing in Pope's imagination ever since reading the elegant jibe of the Earl of Dorset:

> As skilful divers to the bottom fall
> Sooner than those who cannot swim at all;
> So in this way of writing without thinking
> Thou hast a strange alacrity of sinking.[24]

In the *Dunciad* this becomes the invitation of the Goddess to a diving match in Fleet Ditch, an open sewer flowing into the Thames:

> "Here strip my children! here at once leap in!
> "Here prove who best can dash thro' thick and thin,
> "And who the most in love of dirt excel,
> "Or dark dexterity of groping well.
> "Who flings most filth, and wide pollutes around
> "The stream, be his the Weekly Journals, bound.
> "A pig of lead to him who dives the best,
> "A peck of coals a-piece shall glad the rest."

Unhesitatingly, the Dunces dive in: though their styles of sinking vary, their affinity for the medium is the same. The first to 'plunge down-right' is John Dennis (the same who call'd Pope a 'hunchback'd Toad' for the *Essay on Criticism*); next,

> . . . Smedley div'd; slow circles dimpled o'er
> The quaking mud, that clos'd, and ope'd no more.
> All look, all sigh, and call on Smedley lost;
> Smedley in vain resounds thro' all the coast . . .
>   True to the bottom, see Concanen creep,

A cold, long-winded, native of the deep!
If perseverance gain the Diver's prize,
Not everlasting Blackmore this denies:
No noise, no stir, no motion can'st thou make,
Th'unconscious flood sleeps o'er thee like a lake.
　　Not Welsted so: drawn endlong by his scull,
Furious he sinks; precipitately dull.
Whirlpools and storms his circling arm invest,
With all the Might of gravitation blest.
No crab more active in the dirty dance,
Downward to climb, and backward to advance;
He brings up half the bottom on his head,
And boldly claims the Journals and the Lead.
　　　　　　(A. II, 263–70, 279–82, 287–300)

Here, whether sleeping beneath the 'unconscious flood' of excrement, like Conanen, or carrying it aloft, like Welsted, the Dunces are at home in the ultimate realm of Dulness – where man finally abandons himself to decomposition, and his art is what enables him to do it.

5

Reforming the Mind

THE POET AS PHILOSOPHER, 1730

Perhaps no truer comment on the nature of Pope's genius has ever been made than Dr Johnson's – that Pope's mind was

> active, ambitious, and adventurous, always investigating, always aspiring; in its widest searches still longing to go forward, in its highest flights still wishing to be higher; always imagining something greater than it knows, always endeavouring more than it can do.[1]

To possess such a mind is its own punishment, a thought that might have consoled the Dunces, had they known: inherent in it are perpetual restlessness and dissatisfaction with the achievement of the day before; its dreams are Napoleonic, and of their nature incapable of fulfilment. We might suppose that after finishing the *Dunciad*, Pope felt he had completed his major statement on the theme he had spent his life investigating, man's use of art; but from here his mind only leapt to the wider context, the question of man's happiness as a whole, and began to conceive the comprehensive undertaking he came to call, with a conscious reference to Milton, his poem to 'vindicate the ways of God to Man'.[2]

On the publication of the *Dunciad* Pope was aged 40, 'at that exact time of life when years have ripened the judgment, without diminishing the imagination' (as he said of himself, in the persona of the editor);[3] and though he went through more than one cycle of education and assimilation in the course of his life, he does seem to have reached at this time a kind of plateau, from which he could command an extensive field of poetry and philosophy and simultaneously conceive the vast poetic structures into which these could be organised. He experienced the intellectual excitement that every passionate thinker may hope to experience, however briefly, of seeing 'how it all coheres' – and he also experienced the familiar difficulty, of making that radiant conception visible to other eyes than his own. Beneath this was the still more radical difficulty, of determining at what point the structure became too much for the poetry: what simply could not be achieved in verse.

It is a peculiar thought that from this time onwards, Pope considered himself to be committed to a vast work he did not write, of which many apparently unrelated poems are fragments. His aim was nothing less than to tell man who he was and where he belonged in creation, and hence where his true happiness lay. He hoped to explain and reconcile man to his existence in the same breath; as Spence recorded early in 1730, 'Mr. Pope's present design is wholly upon human actions, and to reform the mind.'[4] Nothing could have been more Reasonable, in the deepest sense Pope gave the term. It was also a startlingly rational project, as we see from the description he gave at the end of his life, when it was clear that the poem would never be written:

I had once thought of completing my ethic work in four books. The first, you know, is on the nature of man. The second would have been on knowledge and its limits. Here would have come in an Essay on Education, part of which I have inserted in the *Dunciad*. The third was to have treated of government, both ecclesiastical and civil – and this was what chiefly stopped my going on. I could not have said what I *would* have said without provoking every church on the face of the earth, and I did not care for living always in boiling water. This part would come into my *Brutus*, which is all planned already, and even some of the most material speeches writ in prose. The fourth would have been on morality, in eight or nine of the most concerning branches of it, four of which would have been the two extremes to each of the cardinal virtues.[5]

We may be privately relieved that we do not possess Pope's thoughts on civil and ecclesiastical polity, and the eight or nine chief branches of morality; but nothing could better exemplify a mind 'always imagining something greater than it knows, always endeavouring more than it can do.' Doubtless it was more than prudence that prevented him from making progress with his treatise on government, just as some profound poetical instinct prevented him from writing his blank verse epic, *Brutus*, for all that it was mapped out in prose.[6] But had it not been for vaulting ambition o'erleaping itself, we should not have the *Essay on Man* (corresponding to book one, above), the four *Epistles to Several Persons* (1731–5, saved from the fourth book on morality) – or the satire on contemporary education in the 1742 *Dunciad* (part of book two). These were what Pope could salvage of his vision of the whole; and the rest he reluctantly permitted to escape, as a poet must.[7]

THE *ESSAY ON MAN*, 1733–4

The *Essay* is dedicated to Henry St John Bolingbroke (1678–1751), in companionship with whose volatile, rapid intellect many of its ideas were worked out in 1730. In a letter to their mutual friend, Swift, Bolingbroke calls it a 'noble work which, att my instigation, he has begun', and describes the metaphysical issues the essay grapples with:

> The first Epistle ... considers man, and the Habitation, of man, relatively to the whole system of universal Being, the second ... considers Him in his own Habitation, in Himself, & relatively to his particular system, & the third ... shews how an universal cause
>   works to one end, but works by various laws,
> how Man, & Beast, & vegetable are linked in a mutual Dependancy, parts necessary to each other & necessary to the whole, how human societys were formed, from what spring true Religion and true Policy are derived, how God has made our greatest interest & our plainest Duty indivisibly the same.... [In the fourth epistle, Pope] pleads the cause of God ... against that famous charge which atheists in all ages have brought, the supposed unequal Dispensations of Providence.[8]

When Pope had his vision of 'how it all coheres' he saw that 'Whatever IS, is RIGHT' (I, 294); and the four epistles are really only his editorial attempt to subdivide what was for him a single profound impulse – to submit to the world in which he found himself, and stifle the promptings of pride which would sooner claim that the world itself was out of joint. He was writing out of the same conviction that produced the *Essay on Criticism* ('First follow NATURE') and his characterisation of Achilles' futile, destructive pride; though he was too rational to use such language, it was essentially a mystical vision he wished to communicate, of the world as truly habitable, and worthy of love. If we consider how the *Rape of the Lock* turns on the term 'good Humour', we will not mistake the depth of feeling in Pope's description of his aim to Swift: 'To make mankind look upon this life with comfort and pleasure, and put morality in good humour.'[9]

The value of his vision has been vigorously contested, both in our day and his own. It was received with rapture by a large contemporary audience, before an argument broke out on the Continent about its theology and logic; and it influenced the course of European philosophy (particularly via Kant) even while Johnson was declaring,

> Never were penury of knowledge and vulgarity of sentiment so happily disguised. The reader feels his mind full, though he learns nothing; and when he meets it in its new array no longer knows the talk of his mother and his nurse.[10]

Perhaps the key to such varying responses is not in the content of the essay, but its temper. For Johnson, with his sense of 'a world bursting with sin and sorrow', it was frivolous if not stupid to affirm that 'whatever is, is right'; while poets and thinkers across Europe were increasingly inclined to optimism, whether in the strict sense of Leibniz (*Théodicée*, 1710) or the vaguely happy sense of one of Pope's Dunces, Blackmore:

> See, how the Earth has gain'd that very Place,
> Which of all others in the boundless Space
> Is most Convenient, and will best conduce
> To the wise Ends requir'd for Nature's Use.[11]

The only factors which would irreparably spoil the reader's enjoyment of the poem were a conviction of the supreme reality of pain, like Johnson's, or an addiction to religious orthodoxy and formal logic, such as fuelled the quarrel abroad. Pope might not have resented the imputation that he had merely versified the 'talk of his mother and his nurse', for nothing could have better demonstrated his success in avoiding abstruse speculation, and cleaving to the truths of experience, as he set himself to do.

The subject of the first epistle sounds almost meaningless in the philosophical cant of the period – 'the Nature and State of MAN, with Respect to the UNIVERSAL SYSTEM'[12] – but Pope the poet roots this abstraction in our feelings. What he starts from is the mood that may seize anyone on a clear night, when the infinity of shining stars makes us both marvel at the size of the universe, and despair of understanding it from the spot on which we stand. We seem 'so weak, so little, and so blind' – though even that, says Pope, is a form of pride. We are just what we should be, like everything else:

> Thro' worlds unnumber'd tho' the God be known,
> 'Tis ours to trace him only in our own.
> He, who thro' vast immensity can pierce,
> See worlds on worlds compose one universe,
> Observe how system into system runs,
> What other planets circle other suns,
> What vary'd being peoples ev'ry star,
> May tell why Heav'n has made us as we are.
> But of this frame the bearings, and the ties,
> The strong connections, nice dependencies,
> Gradations just, has thy pervading soul
> Look'd thro'? or can a part contain the whole?
>   Is the great chain, that draws all to agree,
> And drawn supports, upheld by God, or thee?
>   Presumptuous Man! the reason wouldst thou find,
> Why form'd so weak, so little, and so blind!
> First if thou canst, the harder reason guess,
> Why form'd no weaker, blinder, and no less!
> Ask of thy mother earth, why oaks are made
> Taller or stronger than the weeds they shade?
> Or ask of yonder argent fields above,
> Why JOVE's Satellites are less than JOVE?
>   (I, 21–42)

The question 'Why?' in this perspective is a misunderstanding, as erroneous as the incessant queries of childhood. ('Why wasn't I born big? Why does the sun go away?') When man wrestles to understand the universe, he assumes that it has a direct relation to himself that it cannot have. He is part of an ecological whole that Pope conceives of (using the language of the Renaissance) as a 'great chain', rising by fine gradations from the insects and

animals, through man, to God himself. If man is marked out from
the lower orders of existence, it is only by Reason:

> Far as Creation's ample range extends,
> The scale of sensual, mental pow'rs ascends:
> Mark how it mounts, to Man's imperial race,
> From the green myriads in the peopled grass:
> What modes of sight betwixt each wide extreme,
> The mole's dim curtain, and the lynx's beam:
> Of smell, the headlong lioness between,
> And hound sagacious on the tainted green:
> Of hearing, from the life that fills the flood,
> To that which warbles thro' the vernal wood:
> The spider's touch, how exquisitely fine!
> Feels at each thread, and lives along the line:
> In the nice bee, what sense so subtly true
> From pois'nous herbs extracts the healing dew:
> How Instinct varies in the grov'ling swine,
> Compar'd, half-reas'ning elephant, with thine:
> 'Twixt that, and Reason, what a nice barrier;
> For ever sep'rate, yet for ever near! . . .
> The pow'rs of all subdu'd by thee alone,
> Is not thy Reason all these pow'rs in one?
>   (I, 207–24, 231–2)

Pope's evocation of the very sensation of these powers and
instincts, as in the exquisite spidery touch and hesitation of

> Feels at each thread, and lives along the line

is a practical demonstration of the perspective he is advocating.
Each of these forms of life is an end in itself, and in its own way,
perfect. If man is to be as perfect, it must be in fulfilling his own
unique endowment, Reason – which is 'all these pow'rs in one'.
Reason is what enables him both to perceive his relation to the
universe, and accept it unreservedly. Reason is what grasps the
relation of the parts to the whole, as Pope describes it in one of the
most fervid passages he ever wrote:

> All are but parts of one stupendous whole,
> Whose body Nature is, and God the soul;

> That, chang'd thro' all, and yet in all the same,
> Great in the earth, as in th'æthereal frame,
> Warms in the sun, refreshes in the breeze,
> Glows in the stars, and blossoms in the trees,
> Lives thro' all life, extends thro' all extent,
> Spreads undivided, operates unspent,
> Breathes in our soul, informs our mortal part,
> As full, as perfect, in a hair as heart;
> As full, as perfect, in vile Man that mourns,
> As the rapt Seraph that adores and burns;
> To him no high, no low, no great, no small;
> He fills, he bounds, connects, and equals all.
>
> (I, 267–80)

Reason in this sense is a kind of passionate reverence for life-as-it-is; not necessarily a Christian reverence, though Pope uses the word 'God', but a reverence for the force at the centre of life such as any good Buddhist or pantheist might feel. The climactic statement with which the epistle ends, 'Whatever IS, is RIGHT,' reads differently once we hear it as an assertion of this reverence. What, quoted out of context, seems the product of facile optimism, or worse, a dull refusal to admit any doubt at all, now strikes the ear as a statement of faith, the only serious faith Pope possessed: that the right use of Reason is to submit to what is greater than itself:

> All Nature is but Art, unknown to thee;
> All Chance, Direction, which thou canst not see;
> All Discord, Harmony, not understood;
> All partial Evil, universal Good:
> And, spite of Pride, in erring Reason's spite,
> One truth is clear, 'Whatever IS, is RIGHT.'
>
> (I, 289–94)

To call this mysticism is in no sense to deride it, but only to place it in its proper context: not that of logical debate (the *Essay* came badly out of the continental attempt to mount it into a 'système'), but of vision. Mysticism characteristically absorbs opposites into itself, and is unafraid of contradiction. Parts are felt as ministering to the whole, and individual flaws are bathed in the radiance of what they help create. Thus, though the progress of the four

epistles is superficially logical, and traces man through the universe, his inner self, and society, the thrust of the *Essay* lies in lines
that cannot be said to be argued: in Pope's acceptance of the
warring passions, for instance:

> Passions, like Elements, tho' born to fight,
> Yet, mix'd and soften'd, in [God's] work unite: . . .
> Love, Hope, and Joy, fair pleasure's smiling train,
> Hate, Fear and Grief, the family of pain;
> These mix'd with art, and to due bounds confin'd,
> Make and maintain the balance of the mind:
> The lights and shades, whose well accorded strife
> Gives all the strength and colour of our life.
>
> (II, 111–12, 117–22)

Or his repudiation of the complaint that virtue goes unrewarded
while vice wins the prizes of this world:

> What nothing earthly gives, or can destroy,
> The soul's calm sun-shine, and the heart-felt joy,
> Is Virtue's prize: A better would you fix?
> Then give Humility a coach and six,
> Justice a Conq'ror's sword, or Truth a gown,
> Or public Spirit its great cure, a Crown.
>
> (IV, 167–72)

Or his vision of how, through the power of love, man becomes the
mirror image of God himself:

> God loves from Whole to Parts: but human soul
> Must rise from Individual to the Whole.
> Self-love but serves the virtuous mind to wake,
> As the small pebble stirs the peaceful lake;
> The centre mov'd, a circle strait succeeds,
> Another still, and still another spreads.
> Friend, parent, neighbour, first it will embrace,
> His country next, and next all human race,
> Wide and more wide, th'o'erflowings of the mind
> Take ev'ry creature in, of ev'ry kind;
> Earth smiles around, with boundless bounty blest,
> And Heav'n beholds its image in his breast.
>
> (IV, 361–72)

The parallel between the natural expansiveness of love and the easy outward spreading of the ripple, makes this a truly mystical assertion. Man is no longer seen as a battleground of passion and reason, or a creature of sin who must 'rise above' his nature, but as a being whose tendency is naturally Heavenwards, as the ripple's is towards the shore. Searching for his own happiness he finds virtue, and possessing virtue, he generates love – which, at its farthest reach, is indistinguishable from Heaven itself.

A mysticism as highly organised as this, however, raises technical problems in poetry. The faith suffuses the argument to the point where it may not seem to be argument at all; and one may be more sympathetic to Pope's vision than Johnson, without dissenting from his overall objection that 'the reader feels his mind full, though he learns nothing'. The conclusion is, in a sense, foregone; the 'fullness' is the point of the poetry, and the arguments rehearsed are there to be confuted. Perhaps Pope here comes up against the submerged reef on which his 'Opus Magnum' eventually split and sank: the fact that truths (however shining) do not automatically make poetry, and generalisations (however central) do not reach the mind save through closely-realised particulars. He who was normally so sensitive to the difference between truths of fact, and truths of poetry, seems to have succumbed momentarily to the delusion that each guaranteed the other – by which token, Sir Richard Blackmore would also be a poet.

In spite of the paradoxes that fill the *Essay*, therefore, we may find it insufficiently 'crossed' with contradiction to live outside its period: it does not struggle hard enough through the thicket of particulars to reach its general goal. The *Dunciad* is an instructive contrast, where Pope's general meaning is only achieved by breathing life into innumerable particulars, and is all the stronger and more suggestive for it; operating upside-down his mind is at its most poised; while working right-side-up, as in the *Essay*, it is only too much at ease. It is highly unlikely that Pope himself would have accepted this criticism, though, for he considered himself here to have passed a necessary watershed between Fancy and Morality: as he phrases it in his peroration to Bolingbroke,

> Shall then this verse to future age pretend
> Thou wert my guide, philosopher, and friend?
> That urg'd by thee, I turn'd the tuneful art

From sounds to things, from fancy to the heart . . .
                                                   (IV, 389–92)

Nonetheless, when he turned to the next part of his great project, he found himself creating something that in terms of tone and method was implicitly a rebuke to the *Essay on Man*. From shooting at sitting targets, he began to 'shoot at flying game', with a marked increase of excitement and energy.

THE *EPISTLES TO SEVERAL PERSONS* (*MORAL ESSAYS*), 1731–5

The *Epistles to Several Persons* could well be viewed as what 'escaped' from the *Essay on Man*, in both a literal and metaphorical sense. They evolved out of the same nexus of ideas, noted in Pope's conversation by Spence in the summer of 1730,[13] and they were originally intended for the second book of 'Ethic Epistles', of which the *Essay on Man* was the first. The general heading of this book was 'Of the Use of Things', and the poems were indexed in a plan of 1734 as 'Of the Knowledge and Characters of Men', 'Of the particular Characters of Women' and 'Of the Use of Riches'.[14] Later, as Pope's plan grew more grandiloquent, and farther than ever from achievement, they reappeared as part of the fourth book dealing with the opposite extremes of the cardinal virtues, showing prodigality and avarice as the extremes of prudence and illustrating the distinct characters of men and women by way of introduction.[15]

But none of this background makes very much difference to our reading of the poems, and unless prompted by footnotes, we are unlikely to notice the outcroppings of fossilised authorial intention in the reiterated theory of the 'Ruling Passion' (*Essay on Man*, II, 131ff., and *Epistle to Cobham*, 174ff.) or the stress on the interplay of extremes as keeping up 'the Balance of things' (*Essay on Man*, II, 205–6, and *Epistle to Bathurst*, 161–78). Pope's own despair about how to keep these epistles in their proper categories may be, for us, a source of pleasure. The procedural logic of the poems is constantly being overwhelmed by local effects, and unlike the epistles of the *Essay*, which are really discourses addressed to a silent sympathiser, these are truly letters, with all the communicativeness implied.

If we ask where these poems sprang from (as opposed to where

Pope later planned to put them) the answer seems to be, from both art and life: from life, in the sense that each of them is dedicated to a friend, and encapsulates the kind of talk and the habitual subjects Pope shared with that person; and from art, in that under the strain of generating the *Essay on Man*, Pope found himself reaching out for a liberating new literary model: Horace (65–8 BC). The process of borrowing another's tone or method, which in most writers would mark a subterfuge, in Pope almost always yields new energy and conviction, as we have seen from the beginning; and Horace yielded just what he needed at that moment, a way of taking philosophy off its stilts and making it sound as irresistible as common sense. Horace too had written verse letters to friends, on aesthetic and moral topics, and his manner had been spontaneous, pithy and full of shifts of tone. These were the very qualities Pope had found so engaging in Bolingbroke's conversation, and which he had made into the final compliment of the *Essay on Man*, in lines which were virtually a translation of Horace's own aim (*Satire* I, x, 9–14):

> Teach me, like thee, in various nature wise,
> To fall with dignity, with temper rise;
> Form'd by thy converse, happily to steer
> From grave to gay, from lively to severe;
> Correct with spirit, eloquent with ease,
> Intent to reason, or polite to please.
>
> (IV, 377–82)

The Latin lines were eventually placed as an epigraph to all four of the *Epistles*.

Horace had seen what Pope was in the process of discovering – that the writing of effective philosophy was first and foremost a technical problem, of achieving easiness without loss of weight, and authority without dogmatism. 'Steering from grave to gay' liberated the reader's mind into making its own discoveries: the lighter the poet's touch, the deeper the eventual impress. Horace called his satires, indeed, *sermones* ('talks'), where 'talk' applies equally to the style and the content, and each is what makes the other possible. This is the opposite of 'cutting one's coat according to one's cloth', for the moralist's unpretending approach only proves how much he is in earnest. As Pope had long ago phrased it in his Horatian *Essay on Criticism*,

> Men must be *taught* as if you taught them *not*,
> And Things *unknown* propos'd as Things *forgot*:
> Without Good Breeding, Truth is disapprov'd;
> *That* only makes *Superior* Sense *belov'd*.
>
> (574–7)

To guarantee this 'Good Breeding' which makes 'Superior Sense' lovable, Pope addresses his epistles to a friend whose own high qualities are felt by the poet as a kind of discipline: intelligent enough to draw out the poet's best intelligence, severe in judgement, yet worldly-wise, and able to appreciate how sharp characterisations differ from gossip. The secret of teaching men 'as if you taught them not' lies in the attractiveness of the friend's character, which insensibly draws the reader into an alliance with the friend's implied standards; and in embodying Pope's moral in the friend's own practice, so that the final compliment of the poem seems to conceal no design on the reader.

The first of these friends (to take the epistles in their order of composition, rather than their final ordering for the 'Opus Magnum') was Richard Boyle, third Earl of Burlington (1695–1753). Burlington was the leader of the Palladian Revival in England, whose publication of Renaissance designs, based on the careful measurement of classical ruins, provided Englishmen with the purest models for their country houses. While stone continued to curl and turret in rococo forms across the rest of Europe, he made an ideal of proportion, simplicity and fitness, always remembering that taste has its foundation in usefulness rather than opulence ('You show us, Rome was glorious, not profuse,/And pompous buildings once were things of Use.' 23–4) Pope had been on the friendliest terms with Burlington ever since they were neighbours in Chiswick in 1716, and in the epistle we seem to eavesdrop on the conversations they had while Pope was creating his villa and garden in Twickenham. Their shared conviction is that loveliness is always essentially natural – and the best use of art is modestly to disguise itself in the service of nature:

> To build, to plant, whatever you intend,
> To rear the Column, or the Arch to bend,
> To swell the Terras, or to sink the Grot;
> In all, let Nature never be forgot.
> But treat the Goddess like a modest fair,

Nor over-dress, nor leave her wholly bare;
Let not each beauty ev'ry where be spy'd,
Where half the skill is decently to hide.
He gains all points, who pleasingly confounds,
Surprizes, varies, and conceals the Bounds.
(47–56)

The poetry has the mark of Pope's happiest work, of being about several things at once: behind the conception of the role of the landscape artist lies his *Essay on Man* belief in a deity whose created world is supreme art ('All Nature is but Art, unknown to thee'), and behind his theory that surprise, variety and concealment are the key to the visual arts lies the thought that, of course, this applies equally well to poetry, and particularly to the kind of Horatian poetry he is writing. The intelligence of the poem shows in its transitions, rather than its logic: it bounds from point to point, and in the true Horatian manner seals its meaning with anecdote. No positive instructions could convey so much as a living illustration of tasteless magnificence:

At Timon's Villa let us pass a day,
Where all cry out, 'What sums are thrown away!'
(99–100)

Timon's villa has been built on the old model of grandeur first, utility last, epitomised for Pope by Versailles where the palace and gardens are equally repugnant to nature. The purpose of such architecture, and such tight-clipped gardening, is precisely to flaunt how nature has been subdued to man's purposes; not his co-artist who 'paints as you plant, and, as you work, designs' (1.64) but a slave to his whims:

No pleasing Intricacies intervene,
No artful wildness to perplex the scene,
Grove nods at grove, each Alley has a brother,
And half the platform just reflects the other.
The suff'ring eye inverted Nature sees,
Trees cut to Statues, Statues thick as trees,
With here a Fountain, never to be play'd,
And there a Summer-house, that knows no shade . . .
(115–22)

The *Essay on Man* theme that such piled-up greatness is only littleness made manifest ('a great Quarry of Stones above ground', as Pope and his friends said of Blenheim Palace)[16] is carried through in comic detail: Timon's library-books are for show, not reading, his dinner-table is the place where the guests admire, not enjoy, the food, and the whole house is formed for parade, not human existence. But Nature herself will have the last laugh, as Pope shows in a sudden shift of philosophical perspective. What Timon supposes himself to 'own' will revert to bearing corn one day, as if it had never been styled and terraced:

> Another age shall see the golden Ear
> Imbrown the Slope, and nod on the Parterre,
> Deep Harvests bury all his pride has plann'd,
> And laughing Ceres re-assume the land.
>
> (173–6)

The only way of life that will not finally be mocked by Nature is the submissively creative one that Timon is too proud to practise, which makes the country estate itself a form of harvest, and generates plenty for tenants, livestock and neighbours alike. Well-being should ripple outward from the great house and its owner, like the circles of widening love at the end of the *Essay on Man*:

> Who then shall grace, or who improve the Soil?
> Who plants like BATHURST, or who builds like BOYLE.
> 'Tis Use alone that sanctifies Expence,
> And Splendor borrows all her rays from Sense.
>   His Father's Acres who enjoys in peace,
> Or makes his Neighbours glad, if he encrease;
> Whose chearful Tenants bless their yearly toil,
> Yet to their Lord owe more than to the soil;
> Whose ample Lawns are not asham'd to feed
> The milky heifer and deserving steed;
> Whose rising Forests, not for pride or show,
> But future Buildings, future Navies grow:
> Let his plantations stretch from down to down,
> First shade a Country [i.e. estate], and then raise a Town.
>
> (177–90)

The stewardship of land is actually a school of morality, and man puts himself in a right relationship with the universe by being in right relation with his own small corner of it. The abstract philosophy of the *Essay* here puts down its roots where they belong, in human behaviour.

In the epistles to Allen, Lord Bathurst (1733) and Temple, Viscount Cobham (1734), Pope circles round other themes of the *Essay*. *To Bathurst* is subtitled 'Of the *Use* of *Riches*' and argues 'That it is known to few, most falling into one of the extremes, *Avarice* or *Profusion*', which it illustrates by crosscutting from Cotta the miser to Villiers the spendthrift, and from the Man of Ross to Sir Balaam. This is not the most coherent of the poems, and easily falls apart into shining passages – perhaps because the main point is evident, and the dedicatee not the requisite focus of these thoughts for Pope. (Bathurst is praised for keeping to the golden mean, which, if he did, he did on the same scale he did everything else. The Baron was a large man, with large appetites.) The epistle *To Cobham* dwells on the contradictory natures of men, and is tugged in opposite directions by Pope's desire to prove that all characters have, at bottom, a 'ruling passion' – and his admission that nothing could be harder to find. ('Some few Characters plain, but in general confounded, dissembled, or inconsistent . . . Nothing constant and certain but *God* and *Nature*', as he phrases it in the summary, with audible frustration.) Nonetheless, the effort of embracing contradictory positions at the same time, and finding that his own illustrations escape the category he wished to place them in, often releases Pope's best energies, and the epistle has passages both of great gusto, and psychological subtlety. It admits to its own difficulties with good humour:

> Know, God and Nature only are the same:
> In Man, the judgment shoots at flying game,
> A bird of passage! gone as soon as found,
> Now in the Moon, perhaps, now under ground.
>
> (154–7)

It is in the *Epistle to a Lady* (1735), however, that all he has been learning in the other epistles finds its most exquisite application. Here again are the brief, witty portraits shedding light on every facet of the argument, the leaps of tone ('from grave to gay, from lively to severe'), and the ready admission that the philosopher only puts his salt on the tail of a disappearing argument. The characters of women are 'flying game' in the highest degree, the portrait-artist's despair:

> Pictures like these, dear Madam, to design,
> Asks no firm hand, and no unerring line;
> Some wand'ring touch, or some reflected light,
> Some flying stroke alone can hit 'em right:
> For how should equal Colours do the knack?
> Chameleons who can paint in white and black?
>
> (151–6)

This poem has the kind of coherence only the Horatian method makes possible: it follows the admitted illogicality of its subject with loving attention, and generates meaning in spite of itself. Who would dare deduce a 'meaning' from Papillia?

> Papillia, wedded to her coating spark,
> Sighs for the shades – 'How charming is a Park!'
> A Park is purchas'd, but the Fair he sees
> All bath'd in tears – 'Oh odious, odious Trees!'
>
> (37–40)

But Papillia, like all the other women in the poem, is coloured with the tints of Nature herself; and her meaning for the author of the *Essay on Man* is that what escapes his categories is at least as important as what lies sensibly inside them. Though the artist in the poem pretends to despair, we can feel Pope's relish for his subject in the quality of the poetry; it is as delightful as painting Belinda's sylphs all over again:[17]

> Come then, the colours and the ground prepare!
> Dip in the Rainbow, trick her off in Air,
> Chuse a firm Cloud, before it fall, and in it
> Catch, ere she change, the Cynthia of this minute.
>
> (17–20)

There are other reasons why this poem is the most suggestive and coherent of the four. One is that Martha Blount, its dedicatee (too modest to be named as other than 'a Lady'), is the genuine focus of these thoughts for Pope: the disinterested companion who can share a joke against her sex (the opening quip on feminine vapidity is hers, 'Most Women have no Characters at all') and who harmonises all contradictions in her own good nature. She enables Pope to do what the anti-feminine satirist has never done before, to discover that men and women are not irreconcilable opposites after all. Martha makes her sanity out of the same materials men do – but because she is reconciling stronger contradictions, her harmony vibrates at a more perfect pitch. Pope celebrates the dangerous, delightful achievement in the most beautifully-turned compliment of the age, which poises its meaning on the last syllable so lightly that, if Pope could call Martha 'a softer Man', she might equally have replied, 'and you, a firmer Woman':

> Heav'n, when it strives to polish all it can
> Its last best work, but forms a softer Man;
> Picks from each sex, to make its Fav'rite blest,
> Your love of Pleasure, our desire of Rest,
> Blends, in exception to all gen'ral rules,
> Your Taste of Follies, with our Scorn of Fools,
> Reserve with Frankness, Art with Truth ally'd,
> Courage with Softness, Modesty with Pride,
> Fix'd Principles, with Fancy ever new;
> Shakes all together, and produces – You.
>
> (271–80)

Another reason for the greater resonance of this epistle is the length of time its thoughts and images have been gestating. The original poetical template was a juvenile imitation of the Earl of Dorset, called *Phryne* (c.1709):

> Obscure by Birth, renown'd by Crimes,
> Still changing Names, Religions, Climes,
>   At length she turns a Bride:
> In Di'monds, Pearls, and rich Brocades,
> She shines the first of batter'd Jades,
>   And flutters in her Pride.
>
> So have I known those Insects fair,
> (Which curious *Germans* hold so rare,)
>   Still vary Shapes and Dyes;
> Still gain new Titles with new Forms,
> First Grubs obscene, then wriggling Worms,
>   Then painted Butterflies.
>
> (13–24)

The Restoration brutality that affected to see a prostitute in every wife dropped away, but Pope's own fascination with women's butterfly existence remained – the dangerous transition they made from girlhood to marriage, and the discrepancy that was likely to follow between their inner and outer lives, when it was only on condition of being possessed by another that they became their mature selves. The same ideas are explored in the later *Epistle to Miss Blount, with the Works of Voiture* (1712), where Pope actually pleads against the tyranny of marriage for the 'suff'ring Sex', and they clearly underlie much of the poignant comedy of the *Rape of the Lock*, where the transition from chrysalis to butterfly is so dangerous for Belinda that she prefers to postpone it with a fit of hysterics. The severest lines of *To a Lady* are a long-meditated elegy for all those Belindas who reach old age without maturity:

> Pleasures the sex, as children Birds, pursue,
> Still out of reach, yet never out of view,
> Sure, if they catch, to spoil the Toy at most,
> To covet flying, and regret when lost:
> At last, to follies Youth could scarce defend,
> 'Tis half their Age's prudence to pretend;
> Asham'd to own they gave delight before,
> Reduc'd to feign it, when they give no more:
> As Hags hold Sabbaths, less for joy than spight,
> So these, their merry, miserable Night;
> Still round and round the Ghosts of Beauty glide,
> And haunt the places where their Honour dy'd.
> See how the World its Veterans rewards!
> A Youth of frolicks, an old Age of Cards,
> Fair to no purpose, artful to no end,
> Young without Lovers, old without a Friend,
> A Fop their Passion, but their Prize a Sot,
> Alive, ridiculous, and dead, forgot!
>
> (231–48)

But perhaps the deeper reason for the suggestiveness of this epistle is not that it enabled Pope to articulate thoughts he had been refining for decades, but that it enabled him to say something more than he knew, which sprang out of the poem as it was being written. The effort of describing female characters that required to be 'dipped in the Rainbow' for their colouring, and eluded the artist's 'firm hand' and 'unerring line', led him to meditate in the course of the poem on the elusiveness of life itself. The artist is always offering to 'fix' the flux of existence for eternity, to pin the butterfly, wriggling, on the wall; but if he is honest, he admits that the creature is most exquisitely itself at the moment it flutters away – just as life is at its most lifelike when eluding his poem. He gains his end in proportion to his willingess to despair of it, and hence a kind of joy emanates from the repeated rebuffs of the epistle, from the temper tantrums of Silia ('All eyes may see – a Pimple on her nose', (36)) or the dubious morals of Calypso ('Yet ne'er so sure our passion to create,/As when she touch'd the brink of all we hate.' (51–2)). In its mixture of gaiety and bewilderment, ironic poise and intellectual confusion, the poem conveys the very sensation of being alive – and hence something even more precious than the theoretical overview of life Pope offered in the *Essay on Man*.

The epistle also delivers Pope a moment of supreme artistic happiness, in enabling him to set the seal on his love for Martha Blount and his respect for his own art in the same moment. He sees Martha as having been under the protection of Phoebus Apollo, the God of Poetry, from birth:

> Ascendant Phœbus watch'd that hour with care,
> Averted half your Parents simple Pray'r,
> And gave you Beauty, but deny'd the Pelf
> Which buys your sex a Tyrant o'er itself.
> The gen'rous God, who Wit and Gold refines,
> And ripens Spirits as he ripens Mines,
> Kept Dross for Duchesses, the world shall know it,
> To you gave Sense, Good-humour, and a Poet.
> (285–92)

With a smiling double rhyme (appropriately called a 'feminine' one) Pope pays tribute to Martha, himself, and the art of poetry, which will keep Martha alive when Time has done its worst. He will not strike the heroic postures of the sonneteers, but nonetheless he believes, as they do,

> So long as men can breathe, or eyes can see,
> So long lives this, and this gives life to thee.[18]

6

Virtue and Her Friends

From the *Dunciad* onwards, nothing Pope published went un-attended by some kind of outcry. He had so many enemies in Grub Street that each new poem released a flow of bile; and we may sympathise with his contemporaries' sensation of being attacked on all sides – for there was so much poetry, in so many voices, appearing all at once. The philosophical and Horatian epistles have been discussed under separate headings here for the sake of clarity, but in fact they were produced in the same period, along with a new vein of poetry defending Pope's right to satirise his contemporaries at all: the *Imitations of Horace* (1733–8). Between January and May 1733, for instance, Pope published the *Epistle to Bathurst*, his first *Imitation of Horace* and epistles I–III of the *Essay on Man*. This was made possible, not by astonishingly rapid composi-tion, but by Pope's habit of keeping poems by him for lengthy correction, and his careful reading of the market. The *Epistle to Bathurst* had been held back for two years while the outcry raised by *To Burlington* died down; it was ushered in now by the *Imitation of Horace* that defended its method and that of *To Burlington*, and it formed a smokescreen for the appearance of the *Essay on Man*, which Pope was passionately anxious should receive a fair hearing. He issued it anonymously at the time when his audience supposed his major works for the year had already been published, and as a result had the pleasure of being most loudly praised by the Dunces he had most deeply offended ('It is, indeed, above all commenda-tion,' cried Welsted, among others.)[1] Pope relished the absurdity for all it was worth: 'I am as much overpaid this way now, as I was injur'd that way before'.[2]

His previous 'injury' had been the outcry raised by the portrait of Timon in the *Epistle to Burlington* which, though clearly general-ised and applicable to a dozen grandees, had been maliciously interpreted as a satire on the first Duke of Chandos and his conspicuously opulent estate at 'Cannons'. To improve the story, rumour added that Pope had received money from Chandos, anything from £500 to £1000 – and thus the Wasp of Twickenham stood convicted of treachery and ingratitude towards a man who, to make Pope's embarrassment complete, was a friend of Bathurst, Bolingbroke, and Burlington himself. Chandos did not believe the identification, and wrote to Pope to say so while Pope denied it hotly in the papers, but the imputation was much too enjoyable to Pope's enemies to be killed off.

SATIRES AND LIBELS, FRIENDS AND ICONS

It is worth pausing for a moment to consider the factors that lay behind the Timon scandal, because they dogged Pope's satires to the last and darkened his reputation into our own time. Some of them derive from the distinction between 'realism' in poetry and life, and others are traceable to the difference between the artist's 'humanity' and other people's, as described in the introduction. Unless we accept that the artist's role in relation to life is to perpetuate it in a new form – to be able to say of his work, 'so long lives this, and this gives life to thee' – Pope's behaviour is impossible to understand.

The excitement his detractors felt about the identification of Chandos stemmed from the feeling that Pope had disqualified himself from satire by showing himself ungrateful and treacherous; that he was not better, but worse than other people, and therefore his irritating insistence on standards served only to condemn himself. In fact, as we noted in the introduction, it is not to be denied that artists have less 'humanity' than other people, insofar as their minds must necessarily be on their work as well as on the life around them; and, suspended between two worlds with differing versions of morality and realism, they must move between the two as gracefully as they may. In this sense, Pope might as well have been describing Chandos in Timon as not, for though he had never visited 'Cannons', there is no reason to suppose that, if he had, he would have avoided making use of any ludicrous detail he found there on grounds of decency. His grounds for discrimination would have been only the value of the detail: conscience was more requisite in art than in life itself (pleasant though it was to lay claim to both).

While we may grant, then, that the artist's relation to life has a fifth-columnist air of treachery, we cannot concede that it is actually treacherous. The artist is at work on our behalf; and the fact that life is his raw material does not detract either from the value of what he creates (which cannot, clearly, be life itself) or his right to do so. All we can judge is the created work – whether it exists as an organic creation, or is parasitic on the world around it, and therefore fated to pass away. These larger considerations may help us understand why the form the argument took between Pope and the Dunces was over whether Pope's portraits were satires or libels, a confusion he passionately repudiated:

> There is not in the world a greater Error, than that which Fools are so apt to fall into, and Knaves with good reason to incourage, the mistaking a *Satyrist* for a *Libeller*; whereas to a *true Satyrist* nothing is so odious as a *Libeller*, for the same reason as to a man *truly virtuous* nothing is so hateful as a *Hypocrite*.[3]

A libel is odious both on artistic and moral counts: artistic, because its significance is parasitic on life itself, on a known character of status like Chandos; and moral, because libel denigrates its object for the pleasure of doing so, not in the name of moral standards that are common to all. The satirist acts for the sake of health, like a responsible surgeon cutting away at a distempered body; while the libeller merely knifes his victim because he is a bully, and no one can prevent him.

Another factor in the aggression roused by Pope's satires seems to have been a radical confusion between what is 'real' in poetry and what is 'real' in life. We noted in the introduction that the artist has a more elastic sense of reality than the rest of us, and understands that 'truth' is an honorific term his readers bestow on what convinces them – a technical, not an ethical judgement. Life is one thing, art quite another (though, of course, the value of art derives from, and leads back to, life). When the Dunces insisted that Timon must be Chandos, they were really paying a confused tribute to the vividness of the portrait: anything so lifelike must be 'real'. But when they went on to say that it was a travesty of the 'reality' of Chandos, they betrayed their ignorance of the rules of artistic creation to the bottom. How could it be otherwise?

Perhaps the best analogy for Pope's role as an artist is that he was committed to working 'in real life' as a metalworker works in ore. The straightforward facts of reality are as insignificant to the naked eye as ore is while in the ground – to the inattentive, merely grubby rock, but to the artist, the beginning of all else. The artist's role is to melt, refine and shape it, until everyone can recognise it for what it is; and his guide in this is necessarily the truth he is finally representing, which is by no means the truth of the ore as it once was. Everything else falls away from this as irrelevant dross; hence Pope's callousness to facts his subjects often felt to be inseparable from themselves, and his lack of conscience about the uproar his satires caused, however embarrassed he might be humanly. Others might protest that what he created was 'unreal', but Pope's artistic conscience was satisifed that it was as true as it could be – true to its original value, though only his eyes had been sharp enough to perceive it in the original rock. His art was what made life significant. He might have been glad to borrow the famous formulation of Henry James, that

> It is art that *makes* life, makes interest, makes importance . . . and I know of no substitute whatever for the force and beauty of its process.[4]

The process is the same, whether the artist is working on his enemies (the Dunces), a personality known from hearsay (the Man of Ross), or his closest friend – as we can see from the portrait of Martha Blount in *To a Lady*. What Pope alleges of her is, from the little extant evidence of her character, quite untrue: she seems to have been a passionately modest woman whose 'courage' was less active than passive, and whose 'pride' consisted largely in enduring its mortification. As a spinster, she gave herself to her unreliable and demanding family with morbid dedication, and when Pope bequeathed her a life-interest in his estate at his death, he was making her as independent financially as he had tried to make her mentally for the length of their friendship. The portrait in the epistle was an equivalent gesture – but one which she could sabotage, as her modesty demanded, by refusing to allow him to make the dedication public.

Yet it would be simplistic to call the portrait untrue; it is true to a possibility, a possibility Pope glimpsed through Martha. As we see from her opening witticism, there were moments when a cool, disinterested intelligence spoke forth, and her eyes shone with happy irony. If she was not always the free female spirit he celebrates, principled and yet full of fancy, she nonetheless gave Pope the clue to the charm of such a personality; and beyond this we would be wrong to look for confirmation in the world of fact, as we see from other details at the end of the poem. When Pope seems to describe her most closely (Martha's relation to her worldly, handsome and selfish sister was very much that of the moon to the sun) it is in lines first written in 1722, about someone else entirely (ll.253–6, from verses to Mrs Judith Cowper); and the unmarried Martha in the poem has acquired a husband, daughter, and a knack of marital tact (ll.257–64). Clearly, her maiden status and emotional vulnerability were irrelevant to the portrait Pope was creating; what was needed was an outline that would fit many women, and all could freely identify with. Martha has been annihilated in one sense, to be resurrected in another, more lasting one: from living friend, she has been transmuted into public icon.

THE POET AS GOOD MAN: *IMITATIONS OF HORACE*, 1733–8

All this may be easier to assent to than the allied fact, that Pope also transmuted himself into a public icon at this time – a move which later served to blacken his reputation, when Victorian research began to uncover the complex personality he had simplified.[5] His critics, from his own day into ours, have always assumed that his motive for projecting himself so assiduously as a good man in a wicked world was wholly personal. Knowing the deviousness of his heart, he made use of his poetry to project a shining rectitude, runs the argument; but when we have seen how deliberately Pope steered between the truths of art and life, we are unlikely to be content with such a simple view. Though his motive for picking up his pen was undoubtedly the desire to set the public record straight, he could never have made lasting poetry out of advertising his own virtues. If his virtues needed to be asserted, it was because satire itself depended on the presence of a Good Man, to whom the ways of the world were alien; and no figure could be better suited to the role than a poet, living on the edge of the great world, and raising his head out of the great books of the past to comment on the morals of the present. Best of all, he could claim the protection of the satirists of the past, who had been forced to do the same – above all, of Horace, satirist of Rome.

As Pope said, in printing the first of his *Imitations*, 'An Answer from *Horace* was both more full, and of more Dignity, than any I cou'd have made in my own person':[6] more dignified, because it saved Pope from speaking, or being heard to speak, in a merely personal capacity, and fuller, because their joint voice spoke across space and time, as evidence of the very solidarity to which they were appealing. Horace, like Pope, took his cue from the world about him, but his poetry and values persist beyond it (as Pope demonstrated by printing Horace's text alongside his own, for line-by-line comparison). Horatius Flaccus is buried, but 'Horace' is perfectly alive in the poetry; the Roman quarrels that provoked him are untraceable, but 'Rome' and 'Fannius' are there in the art; and the values the poet was defending have outlasted his culture, just as he knew they would. (Horace himself had them from Greek civilisation, and would not have been surprised to find them sheltering now in the foggy north-west of the Empire, under Hadrian's Wall.) When Pope imitates Horace, following the line of the satires but substituting English personalities for Roman ones, he is demonstrating at every turn the triumph of their shared values over transience. What Horace called virtue is still virtue, and the satirist's duty is still to defend it. What is more he must still proceed as Horace did, by transmuting himself, his friends, and his quarrels into the matter of poetry, and sinking their specific natures to resuscitate them as glowing generalities. This kind of satire grows out of real life, and addresses itself to real life – that is its urgency; but its nature is not life, but art: the art that '*makes* life, makes interest, makes importance.'

The perfection of the 'fit' between Horace's predicament and Pope's shows in the swiftness of the satires' composition. Bolingbroke found Pope confined to his room with a fever in late January 1733, and as he turned over the pages of his bedside-Horace happened on the first satire of the second book. As Pope told Spence, 'He observed how well that would hit my case, if I were to imitate it in English. After he was gone, I read it over, translated it in a morning or two, and sent it to the press in a week or fortnight after'[7] – unheard-of rapidity for Pope. What he found in the satire was the opportunity to defend himself on two vital counts: firstly, that the satirist's motive is not personal bile, and secondly, that he is the keeper of something society cannot do without, a moral 'gold standard'.

He borrows Horace's witty notion of inviting us to eavesdrop on an anxious consultation with his lawyer, Fortescue. This inoffensive satirist is astonished at the annoyance he has given:

> P.   There are (I scarce can think it, but am told)
> There are to whom my Satire seems too bold . . .
>   (1–2)

but when his worldly lawyer bluntly advises him to 'write no
more', the satirist pleads that it is he who is the victim:

> P. Not write? but then I *think*,
> And for my Soul I cannot sleep a wink.
> I nod in Company, I wake at Night,
> Fools rush into my Head, and so I write.
>   (11–14)

Satire becomes an irresistible force that makes use of him, rather
than the other way round. All the rational arguments the lawyer
can put forward fall short of a case presented in such natural
terms: if Pope's vocation is satire, he cannot lend his pen to
praising the Court, profitable though it might be. But the cost is
much higher than he supposes: 'Ev'n those you touch not, hate
you (41).' Pope's plea, however, remains the same: what he does is
natural, and brings its own satisfaction with it, just like the appetite
for eating and drinking – which nobody decries:

> P. Each Mortal has his Pleasure: None deny
> *Scarsdale* his Bottle, *Darty* his Ham-Pye; . . .
> I love to pour out all myself, as plain
> As downright *Shippen*, or as old *Montagne*.
> In them, as certain to be lov'd as seen,
> The Soul stood forth, nor kept a Thought within;
> In me, what Spots (for Spots I have) appear
> Will prove at least the Medium must be clear.
> In this impartial Glass, my Muse intends
> Fair to expose myself, my Foes, my Friends . . .
>   (45–6, 51–8)

This is the heart of his defence: what others call satire is the
spontaneous overflow of natural indignation, such as all large
souls have always experienced. It is so far from an expression of
malice, that the satirist freely offers himself for scrutiny in the same

mirror. His own flaws ('for Spots I have') are the best proof of the honesty of the proceeding: what marks him out is not his unnatural purity, but his openness to criticism. He is free to speak without defensiveness ('I love to pour out all myself'), secure in the conviction that what he is expressing is more than 'self'.

As Pope warms to his theme and asserts his intention to 'Rhyme and Print' in the teeth of all opposition, Fortescue laments what, in that case, will be a short existence – and Pope's rhetoric rises to the proudest assertion of the dignity of the satirist's role he has made. We see how firmly he is rooted in the timeless medium of values supplied by Horace, when the poetry vibrates with an indignation fortified by the examples of Rome, France and England; all of them urging Pope forward, with only this difference, that he is freer to speak than any satirist has ever been:

> P. What? arm'd for *Virtue* when I point the Pen,
> Brand the bold Front of shameless, guilty Men,
> Dash the proud Gamester in his gilded Car,
> Bare the mean Heart that lurks beneath a Star;
> Can there be wanting to defend Her Cause,
> Lights of the Church, or Guardians of the Laws?
> Could pension'd *Boileau* lash in honest Strain
> Flatt'rers and Bigots ev'n in *Louis'* Reign?
> Could Laureate *Dryden* Pimp and Fry'r engage,
> Yet neither *Charles* nor *James* be in a Rage?
> And I not strip the Gilding off a Knave,
> Un-plac'd, un-pension'd, no Man's Heir, or Slave?
> I will, or perish in the gen'rous Cause.
> Hear this, and tremble! you, who 'scape the Laws.
> Yes, while I live, no rich or noble knave
> Shall walk the World, in credit, to his grave.
> TO VIRTUE ONLY and HER FRIENDS, A FRIEND,
> The World beside may murmur, or commend.
>   (105–22)

Pope prints in capitals the line to which, as he reads it, the whole of Horace's satire is tending: the satirist is keeper of the 'gold standard', incorruptible and correspondingly severe – 'to Virtue only and Her Friends, a Friend'. He tries the metal of public currency and calls debased coinage by its true name; he wields the only brand that 'shameless, guilty Men' will shrink from. To have such power it is necessary to be above suspicion oneself, and thanks to his pen and public, thanks even to his Catholicism and bad health, Pope can describe himself as not even Boileau or Dryden could: 'Un-plac'd, un-pension'd, no Man's Heir, or Slave.' In this happy state of liberty he freely chooses the service of 'Virtue and Her Friends', promoting goodness wherever he finds it, and calling virtue by her proper name, as his own friends will when they find it in him. Friendship in this sense is as creative as writing poetry itself – it is life shaped, and made significant, by culture. The life the poet actually lives becomes the paradigm of all his poetry would protect; which is why Pope ends the satire with a glimpse of his world at Twickenham, where love and trust irradiate the dinner table, and displaced statesmen (St John Bolingbroke) and redundant soldiers (Peterborough) relax into their truest selves:

> There *St. John* mingles with my friendly Bowl,
> The Feast of Reason, and the Flow of Soul,
> And He, whose Lightning pierc'd th' *Iberian* Lines,
> Now, forms my Quincunx, and now ranks my Vines.
> (127–30)

He lives among the great as an equal, not as a parasite:

> *Envy* must own, I live among the Great,
> No Pimp of Pleasure, and no Spy of State,
> With Eyes that pry not, Tongue that ne'er repeats,
> Fond to spread Friendships, but to cover Heats,
> To help who want, to forward who excel;
> This, all who know me, know; who love me, tell;
> And who unknown defame me, let them be
> Scriblers or Peers, alike are *Mob* to me.
> This is my Plea, on this I rest my Cause –
> What saith my Council learned in the Laws?
> (133–42)

'This is my Plea' – that in his life as in his work, the poet creates in obedience to a higher law than the lawyer normally interprets. Those Yahoos who cannot understand, who pull down as unremittingly as the poet builds, are beyond his concern:

And who unknown defame me, let them be
Scriblers or Peers, alike are *Mob* to me.

If we are curious to know what kind of defamation Pope was braving in lines like these, a pamphlet published the following month is a good example:

If Limbs unbroken, Skin without a Stain,
Unwhipt, unblanketed, unkick'd, unslain;
That wretched little Carcase you retain:
The Reason is, not, that the World wants Eyes;
But thou'rt so mean, they see, and they despise.

The violent diatribe ends with a curse:

Like the first bold Assassin's be thy Lot,
Ne'er be thy Guilt forgiven, or forgot;
But as thou hate'st, be hated by Mankind,
And with the Emblem of thy crooked Mind,
Mark'd on thy Back, like *Cain*, by God's own Hand;
Wander like him, accursed through the Land.[8]

The author was Lady Mary Wortley Montagu, once the object of Pope's gallantry and witty correspondence, and now – along with her ally, Lord Hervey – his most heartfelt enemy, for reasons we can only guess at.[9] Whatever they were, they sufficed to make Pope, on his side, forget his rule that all persons mentioned in a satire should have wider significance than themselves, and harry her through the length of the satires under the name of Sappho (in the *Imitation* he had written, 'From furious *Sappho* scarce a milder Fate,/P——x'd by her Love, or libelled by her Hate', 83–4); and on her side, to make her print these *Verses Address'd to the Imitator of the First Satire of the Second Book of Horace*, in which she libels him as extensively as he anticipated – his satire, deformity, obscure birth, misanthropy, weakness, cowardice and conceit. When Lord Hervey joined her later in the year with a feeble satire on the derivativeness of Pope's works, Pope was goaded into a carefully dignified reply in prose, *A Letter to a Noble Lord*.

Why had he been forced to discontinue Hervey's and Lady Mary's acquaintance? Because they were aristocrats in status but not in essentials; and the freedoms they laid claim to were not freedoms he could use:

> I assure you my reason for so doing, was merely that you had both *too much wit* for me; and that I could not do, with *mine*, many things which you could do with *yours*.[10]

This letter he finally decided to suppress, but the pain and anger generated by the affair found another outlet in welding together a number of fragments that had been accumulating in his drawers.[11] These became the *Epistle to Dr Arbuthnot*, published in 1735: the most freestanding of all his satires, and an imitation of Horace only in the sense of growing, like Horace's own works, out of a nexus of thoughts about life and art, truth and treachery, enmity and the way to respond to it. As in the first Imitation, there are the same stratagems of contrast, and the same insistence that in the poet, public and private virtue is the same; but now there is additional stress on the absurdity, and even horror, of the corruption of the best in society, when the traitors turn out to be those in the first rank – the freest and most gifted, those in the best position to do damage.

Pope's thoughts about Lady Mary and Lord Hervey took his mind back to Joseph Addison, now dead, and his behaviour in 1715, when he had managed to welcome Pope's *Iliad* and Tickell's rival translation at the same time. The urbane hypocrisy Addison had shown, and the perversion of his judgement (chiefly on political grounds: he had instigated Tickell's 'Whig' translation) were lessons Pope had not needed to learn twice. The satirical portrait he had drawn at the time now re-emerges in the *Epistle* as an archetype of civilised treachery. It is not possible to be 'keeper of the gold standard' without the courage to stand and defend it; and critical values that do not oblige the critic to welcome the best, wherever it may derive from, merely confirm the self in its own limitations. All Addison's charm and intelligence – and Pope has felt them as deeply as anyone – only make the betrayal more disturbing:

> Peace to all such! but were there One whose fires
> True Genius kindles, and fair Fame inspires,
> Blest with each Talent and each Art to please,
> And born to write, converse, and live with ease:

Shou'd such a man, too fond to rule alone,
Bear, like the *Turk*, no brother near the throne,
View him with scornful, yet with jealous eyes,
And hate for Arts that caus'd himself to rise;
Damn with faint praise, assent with civil leer,
And without sneering, teach the rest to sneer;
Willing to wound, and yet afraid to strike,
Just hint a fault, and hesitate dislike;
Alike reserv'd to blame, or to commend,
A tim'rous foe, and a suspicious friend,
Dreading ev'n fools, by Flatterers besieg'd,
And so obliging that he ne'er oblig'd;
Like *Cato*, give his little Senate laws,
And sit attentive to his own applause;
While Wits and Templers ev'ry sentence raise,
And wonder with a foolish face of praise.
Who but must laugh, if such a man there be?
Who would not weep, if *Atticus* were he!
                                        (193–214)

It is all the result of want of courage: Addison's vanity is such that anyone can damage it and all must contribute to its upkeep, and the automatic distrust of distinction in others which emerges in his damning praise, transmits itself through the rest of his clique by osmosis. No talents can flourish, unrooted in anything more sustaining than anxious self-regard; and Addison's are stunted into triviality by his own weakness. But there are consequences for society, too, and this Cato of the coffee houses betrays his obligations as a critic towards emerging talent in the most degrading way. It is just when he is needed that Addison goes missing: 'Damn with faint praise, assent with civil leer,/And without sneering, teach the rest to sneer'.

It is another version of this slipperiness that Pope analyses in Sporus, his generalised portrait of Lord Hervey (1696–1743). What in Addison, however, was a failure of nerve, in Hervey is the falsity of every breath he draws. He has not even made the primary decision of committing himself to one sex more than another. (Hervey was exceptionally pretty, and his equally pretty wife was apparently chosen to create a matching set. Fortunately, she made no objection to his giving most of his passion to male lovers.) This ambiguous creature, whom Pope names Sporus, for the courtier

Nero castrated and called his 'wife', flourishes at court as naturally as all rootless, power-sensitive organisms do. Power needs courtiers, as courtiers seek power: Walpole found Hervey a useful tool, and Hervey made his career as Vice-Chamberlain to the King's Household out of Walpole's ascendancy.

Pope had not always seen Hervey in so harsh a light. When he kept company in London with aristocrats and wits, Hervey had been among them, as had his wife-to-be, Mary Lepell, and Lady Mary herself. But in the 1720s these friendships had dwindled away, perhaps for the reason Pope gave in his letter, that these aristocrats felt able to do many things with their wit that he could not do with his – their laughter was higher-pitched because it knew no boundaries, and more corrosive, because it admitted no constructive meaning. Certainly Hervey's *Memoirs of the Reign of King George II* give us an uncomfortable insight into what he made of his gifts. It is a lucid and intelligent account of a stultifying situation, prized by historians and anecdotalists alike (his account of a royal evening is almost a version of the court of Dulness).[12] But at the same time that Hervey exposes the motives of others with urbane cynicism, he reveals himself as the gigolo of a doting Queen Caroline, manipulating this manipulator of the King by reporting lies and rumours at will.[13] He blushes at nothing, because he sees nothing to blush at; throughout the *Memoir* he seems to dimple at the reader and announce, 'This is how I survive – and how do you?'

There is, apparently, a kind of intelligence which guarantees nothing, a freedom which slips into deliquescence, and a kind of humanity which yearns to regress. In Hervey, evolution is invited to slide backward, and in Pope's satire he reverts from the noble posture of man, erect on two legs, to that of a reptile gliding on its belly, by the various stages of gilded bug, fawning spaniel, and toad:

> Let *Sporus* tremble – 'What, that Thing of silk,
> *Sporus*, that mere white Curd of Ass's milk?
> Satire or Sense, alas! can *Sporus* feel?
> Who breaks a Butterfly upon a Wheel?'
> Yet let me flap this Bug with gilded wings,
> This painted Child of Dirt that stinks and stings;
> Whose Buzz the Witty and the Fair annoys,

Yet Wit ne'er tastes, and Beauty ne'er enjoys,
So well-bred Spaniels civilly delight
In mumbling of the Game they dare not bite.
Eternal Smiles his Emptiness betray,
As shallow streams run dimpling all the way.
Whether in florid Impotence he speaks,
And, as the Prompter breathes, the Puppet squeaks;
Or at the Ear of *Eve*, familiar Toad,
Half Froth, half Venom, spits himself abroad,
In Puns, or Politicks, or Tales, or Lyes,
Or Spite, or Smut, or Rymes, or Blasphemies.
His Wit all see-saw between *that* and *this*,
Now high, now low, now Master up, now Miss,
And he himself one vile Antithesis.
Amphibious Thing! that acting either Part,
The trifling Head, or the corrupted Heart!
Fop at the Toilet, Flatt'rer at the Board,
Now trips a Lady, and now struts a Lord.
Eve's Tempter thus the Rabbins have exprest,
A Cherub's face, a Reptile all the rest;
Beauty that shocks you, Parts that none will trust,
Wit that can creep, and Pride that licks the dust.

(305–33)

There could be no better demonstration of the truth that, while poets may feel as other people, they do different things with their feelings. What hatred Pope undoubtedly felt for Hervey is here held steady by a power of attention, and a curiosity about details, that are much more devastating than hatred. The central charge, that Sporus is an 'amphibious Thing', unites the imagery ('Half Froth, half Venom') and the facts of his existence (his parliamentary career as Walpole's 'puppet', his court role at the 'ear of *Eve*', his marriage) – before reaching its climax in the central icon of Christian evil, the serpent in the garden: 'A Cherub's face, a Reptile all the rest'. And this radical contempt on natural, cultural, and moral grounds of all Sporus is, Pope holds in balance with a free admission of all he might have been:

Beauty that shocks you, Parts that none will trust,
Wit that can creep, and Pride that licks the dust.

To be able to hate so vigorously without becoming the prisoner of one's own hatred, and to have a concept of a moral civilisation which throws off 'amphibiousness' in all its many forms, is a high kind of freedom; and may help us grasp why Pope sets against Hervey's grovelling sinuousness the liberty of himself as a satirist. The satirist is nobody's tool, and his happiness is of the securest kind – of being without vanity, and consciously in service of something greater than himself. This is a freedom available to any human being, but one the timid Addison and supple Hervey will never experience:

> Not Fortune's Worshipper, nor Fashion's Fool,
> Not Lucre's Madman, nor Ambition's Tool,
> Not proud, nor servile, be one Poet's praise
> That, if he pleas'd, he pleas'd by manly ways;
> That Flatt'ry, ev'n to Kings, he held a shame,
> And thought a Lye in Verse or Prose the same:
> That not in Fancy's Maze he wander'd long,
> But stoop'd to Truth, and moraliz'd his song:
> That not for Fame, but Virtue's better end,
> He stood the furious Foe, the timid Friend,
> The damning Critic, half-approving Wit,
> The Coxcomb hit, or fearing to be hit;
> Laugh'd at the loss of Friends he never had,
> The dull, the proud, the wicked, and the mad;
> The distant Threats of Vengeance on his head,
> The Blow unfelt, the Tear he never shed;
> The Tale reviv'd, the Lye so oft o'erthrown;
> Th' imputed Trash, and Dulness not his own;
> The Morals blacken'd when the Writings scape;
> The libel'd Person, and the pictur'd Shape;
> Abuse on all he lov'd, or lov'd him, spread,
> A Friend in Exile, or a Father, dead;
> The Whisper that to Greatness still too near,
> Perhaps, yet vibrates on his SOVEREIGN's Ear –
> Welcome for thee, fair Virtue! all the past:
> For thee, fair Virtue! welcome ev'n the *last!*
>
>   (334–59)

'PRINTING PRIVATE LETTERS', 1735–7

On this heady note of scorn and liberty it may be timely to turn to the story of Pope's private correspondence, which so scandalised his Victorian editor, Reverend Elwin. The poet-hero who 'thought a Lye in Verse or Prose the same' proved so overwhelmingly lifelike to posterity that he was taken for the real Pope, and it was the very nobility of his stance as a satirist that provoked the Reverend's denunciation of his 'rascality':

> Either the guilty appearances are deceptive, or we must admit that his mind was essentially corrupt. His correspondence brings up the ever-recurring enquiry, and we have to decide whether his letters are not many of them fraudulent, and the circumstances attending their publication a series of ignominious plots, infamous false accusations, and impudent lies.[14]

If the real Pope did think a lie in verse or prose the same, it was only in the sense that, if truth in verse was a technical issue, lies in prose that helped support his verse were also basically technical: all part of the Pope he was creating that was more than self. As we have seen in his treatment of personalities in the *Epistles to Several Persons*, he had no hope that mere reality – a naked, shivering, inartistic thing – would survive in his poetry down the generations. What was needed was a truer truth, a reality purged, hardened and beaten into shape like metal; and when he came to apply the process to himself, he did it with the same artistic detachment, and the same pertinacity, he applied to the rest of mankind. The only respect in which he overreached himself was in supposing that the world would confine its attention to the truth he was showing it, and not enquire with fascination into the inartistic reality behind.

What the Reverend Elwin found so unpardonable in Pope's behaviour was that he had contrived to have his private letters published by the pirate bookseller, Curll, in 1735 – in order to be able to publish an authoritative version in self-defence shortly after, with this denunciation of Curll's proceeding:

> The printing private letters in such a manner, is the worst sort of *betraying Conversation*, as it has evidently the most extensive, and the most lasting ill consequences. It is the highest offence against

Society, as it renders the most dear and intimate intercourse of friend with friend, and the most necessary commerce of man with man, unsafe, and to be dreaded. To open Letters is esteem'd the greatest breach of honour; even to look into them already open'd or accidentally dropt, is held an ungenerous, if not an immoral act. What then can be thought of the procuring them merely by Fraud, and the printing them merely for Lucre?[15]

If we had reproached Pope at the time for telling such a barefaced lie in print, we can be sure he would have arched both eyebrows at us and found no difficulty in justifying himself (that is, if he had opened his lips at all). In the first place, it was no kind of lie to deplore Curll's publishing methods, which were tantamount to robbery. He persistently published materials obtained by bribery or theft without the author's permission, and had already printed some of Pope's early correspondence with Henry Cromwell in just this way. Secondly, he had advertised in 1733 for any material anyone might wish to sell him, with a view to writing an unauthorised *Life of Pope* – one of that series of *Lives*, Arbuthnot quipped, which had added a new terror to death. Pope had simply supplied him with some unusually authoritative material. And thirdly, it was an exquisite joke to make Curll's repulsive habits the instrument, not only of his own undoing, but of Pope's most urgent need of the moment, which was to get his own correspondence into print without seeming to wish it. Were we quite impervious to humour?

It was the old problem of the rules of art and life again: in life, it was still frowned on in 1735 to make private letters public, and it was quite unthinkable for a gentleman to publish such things – while in art, it was a genre at which many of Pope's heroes had excelled, and when performed by Romans (Cicero or Pliny) and Frenchmen (Voiture or Balzac) was acknowledged to be entertaining in the extreme. Considering himself to belong to the history of art, as Pope did, he saw no reason not to add his correspondence to his collected works.[16] (These were augmented in 1735 by a Volume II, containing his poetry from the *Dunciad* onwards in the same formats as his Volume I and the eleven volumes of Homer.) If the price of achieving this was an elaborate fiction involving newspaper advertisements, ghostly go-betweens named 'P.T.' and 'R.S.', and even at one point the House of Lords, it was one Pope willingly paid – and all the more freely because of his sense of how in poetry, it was only art that made life truly lifelike.[17] (It must be said, however, that he proved to have overestimated his powers beyond the printed page. Curll was not wholly deceived, and loudly proclaimed the fraud after publishing the correspondence; while perspicacious contemporaries guessed what had happened, and reproached Pope for his 'juggling': 'In Publick 'gainst the Deed you bawl;/You CURLL, and CURLL you Villain, call.')[18]

Pope had a second motive for this elaborate chicanery, however, as urgent as his artistic respect for his own productions. Curll's advertisement for unauthorised materials with which to concoct a *Life*, as libellous as he wished, coincided with the scandals surrounding Pope's Horatian epistles and all the attendant slurs on his shape, origins and temper. It had never been so urgent to establish that he was, in fact, a normal human being, tender to his parents and friends and as benevolent towards his enemies as they permitted him to be. The beauty of his correspondence was that – particularly printed against his will – it could make this image seem wholly unstudied. As he said of the letters in his own edition:

> Many of them having been written on the most trying occurrences, and all in openness of friendship, are a proof what were his real Sentiments, as they flow'd warm from the heart, and fresh from the occasion; without the least thought that ever the world should be witness to them. Had he sate down with a design to draw his own Picture, he could not have done it so truly; for whoever sits for it (whether to himself or another) will inevitably find the features more compos'd, than his appear in these letters.[19]

Thus the correspondence was designed to do the same work as the *Imitations of Horace*, and the *Epistle to Dr Arbuthnot*: to project the satirist as an inoffensive human being in a wicked world. And in spite of Pope's protestations above, he did it by the same application of art to life. This intermixture was another of the things that scandalised the Reverend Elwin: for it proved impossible to conjure up the actual correspondence of twenty years before, particularly the letters addressed to the dead great (like Congreve, to whom Pope had dedicated the *Iliad*) or the dead and estranged (like Addison). A small portion of the correspondence required to be knitted together from letters of the same period that Pope had been able to retrieve – a stratagem that has cast radical doubt on all the rest. But it does not seem that the letters as a whole are untrustworthy, and the many subsequent finds, which have swelled his correspondence to five volumes, do not significantly alter the portrait Pope gave in his. In printing the letters, Pope altered the punctuation and made improvements to the style, as we should expect; but even more importantly, he had conceived them artistically in the first place. Their spontaneity itself – what Pope liked to call 'the very *déshabille* of the understanding'[20] – was an artistic stratagem, and we would search them in vain for an unguarded revelation or discordant outburst, as posterity has noted with some irritation. ('Mr. Pope laboured his letters as much as the *Essay on Man*, and as they were written to everybody, they do not look as if they had been written to anybody', was Horace Walpole's judgement.)[21]

Certainly the correspondence gives us no glimpse of Pope as he must have sounded talking to himself: the Pope who plotted with such dedication against Curll, the Pope who saw himself in the mirror after being caricatured as a monkey or spider, the Pope who despised the anxious vanity of petty authors but could not tell them so (though we may read between the lines of his correspondence with Broome or Aaron Hill), or the professional Pope who, 'lest he should lose a thought', called a domestic from her bed 'four times in one night, to supply him with paper.'[22] The Pope displayed in the letters is not an invented character, but a selective one, whose virtues are shown without the complex psychological subsoil in which they grew, and the accompanying tension. He is not the artistic fifth-columnist here, but the normal human being whose first loyalty is to his friends. He is responsive to their moods and opinions, careful not to obtrude his physical or emotional needs, and (no invention, this) indefatigable in his charities towards them. If the artist shows through, it is in the high polish of particular setpieces, like the comic account of a ride to Oxford with Lintot, or the conscious philosophy of his thoughts on sickness.[23] Otherwise he portrays himself as a man among men: respectful in his early friendship with Wycherley, a gay dog with Henry Cromwell, gallant to young ladies, wronged but dignified in his relations with Addison, humble towards Greek scholars, and pious and proper among his Catholic friends. The tones are many, but the overall impression is, as Johnson says, 'a perpetual and unclouded effulgence of general benevolence, and particular fondness. There is nothing but liberality, gratitude, constancy, and tenderness.' (He went on to say, 'There is, indeed, no transaction which offers stronger temptations to fallacy and sophistication than epistolary intercourse . . .'.)[24]

The artistic respect Pope felt for his own correspondence, and the hopes he nursed in publishing it, were abundantly justified by the public reception: between authoritative reprints and pirated ones, it ran through more than thirty editions, and helped remove for good the stigma that attached to the printing of private letters. It also made him as much a public icon as he had helped to make his friends. Doubtless Ralph Allen (model for Fielding's upright Squire Allworthy in *Tom Jones*) was not the only reader to feel he now understood Pope's nature as never before. Though he had long admired him 'for the excellence of his genius' (as Pope's first biographer puts it),

> The asperity of his satirical pieces was so repugnant to the softness and suavity of that worthy man's disposition, that it in some degree estranged him from his intimacy. But no sooner had he read over our author's letters, than he loved him for the goodness and virtues of his heart.[25]

EPILOGUE TO THE SATIRES, 1738

Pope continued to imitate Horace while preparing his correspondence (and while laying an even more elaborate scheme for retrieving his correspondence from Swift in Ireland, eventually to be published 'without' his intervention in 1741). There followed, in 1734, imitations of *Satire II, ii* and *Sermo I, ii* (a piece of mischief this, a diatribe on London's sexual mores that had to be printed anonymously), in 1737 *Epistle II, ii* and an exquisitely ironic address to George II, *Epistle II, i*, mingling literary history with an increasingly dangerous disgust for kings.[26] In 1738 Pope printed another epistle expressing his love and admiration for Bolingbroke (*Epistle I, i*) and a tender adaptation of the satire on the Town and Country Mouse, prepared with, and in the style of, Swift (*Satire II, vi*). From the number of these imitations and the rapidity of their preparation, it is clear that Pope had opened a Horatian vein he could have exploited to the end. Perhaps, too, they may raise the suspicion we have voiced before, that what puts up no resistance to Pope does not elicit his finest writing. 'What is easy is seldom excellent', says Johnson, majestically, of these imitations,[27] and while they have shining and much-quoted paragraphs, they do not often tell us more than we could have deduced from the two satires discussed above.

In 1738, however, Pope printed two highly political dialogues in support of the Opposition, which supply a suggestive background to his last revision of the *Dunciad* (1742–3). The key political fact of English life since 1721 had been the reign of Walpole as chief minister – the man who cheerfully proclaimed himself 'no Saint, no Spartan, no Reformer', and maintained the stability of his reign by opposition to parliamentary reform, and such liberal abuse of the patronage system that, as Pope phrases it, 'Not to be corrupted [was] the Shame'. Walpole's pragmatism has been viewed rather comfortably by recent historians (his method of paying for political services, and debauching troublesome idealists in advance, was efficient in its way), but the experience of living amidst it was another thing. Anyone with a notion of disinterested action in public life was bound to be in opposition to Walpole, even without being the devoted friend of Bolingbroke – author of the Opposition paper *The Craftsman*, and organiser of parliamentary resistance to Walpole in the Excise Crisis of 1733. Pope's public identification with Bolingbroke had grown all the stronger during the 1730s, at no small political risk to himself, and the two dialogues are a despairing swansong on the prevailing atmosphere – as Pope writes in a note to the concluding line:

> This was the last poem of the kind printed by our author, with a resolution to publish no more; but to enter thus, in the most plain and solemn manner he could, a sort of PROTEST against that insuperable corruption and depravity of manners, which he had been so unhappy as to live to see. Could he have hoped to have amended any, he had continued those attacks; but bad men were grown so shameless and so powerful, that Ridicule was become as unsafe as it was ineffectual.

The most celebrated passage in the dialogues at the time, and since, is Pope's vision of the Triumph of Vice – a sonorous orchestration of the collapse of public values that has more than one thing in common with the vision of encroaching darkness at the end of the *Dunciad*:

Lo! at the Wheels of her Triumphal Car,
Old *England*'s Genius, rough with many a Scar,
Dragg'd in the Dust! his Arms hang idly round,
His Flag inverted trails along the ground!
Our Youth, all liv'ry'd o'er with foreign Gold,
Before her dance; behind her crawl the Old!
See thronging Millions to the Pagod run,
And offer Country, Parent, Wife, or Son!
Hear her black Trumpet thro' the Land proclaim,
That 'Not to be corrupted is the Shame.'
In Soldier, Churchman, Patriot, Man in Pow'r,
'Tis Av'rice all, Ambition is no more!
See, all our Nobles begging to be Slaves!
See, all our Fools aspiring to be Knaves!
The Wit of Cheats, the Courage of a Whore,
Are what ten thousand envy and adore.
All, all look up, with reverential Awe,
On Crimes that scape, or triumph o'er the Law:
While Truth, Worth, Wisdom, daily they decry –
'Nothing is Sacred now but Villainy.'

Yet may this Verse (if such a Verse remain)
Show there was one who held it in disdain.
                              (*Dialogue* I, 151–72)

7

The Progress of Dulness

The encroaching dark for Pope was lit with the gleam of something brazen – the gleam of effrontery, fully at ease with itself, as it flourished under the patronage of Walpole (*alias* Sir Robert Brass). It was this cheap new source of illumination, flashing brassily upon him from many quarters, that began to fix his thoughts on the *Dunciad* again. He had already explored the paradoxes of flying lead and uncreating words, the passion for plunging to the poetical depths, but this was something new, without the hint of bathos he had found in 1728. The brazen shine now worn by public life was impervious to shame: it glowed in triumph.

But it is a nice example of how repeatedly in Pope's career his poems formed themselves under cover of other projects, that he did not suppose himself to be preparing for a reworking of the *Dunciad* at all in these last years. Though it seems to us inevitable that the last great project of his life would involve closing a circle of creativity, and loading old rifts with new ore, his conscious mind was still worrying away at uncompleted projects. The 'Opus Magnum', whose third book on civil and ecclesiastical government he had dropped because he did not 'care for always living in boiling water' (p. 98 above), was now giving rise to the idea of an epic poem – a poem on the (mythic) civilising mission of the Trojan Brutus to Britain, which would accommodate his thoughts on government and religion in a less contentious guise. He described it confidently to Spence in 1743:

> The plan of government is much like our old original plan, supposed so much earlier, and the religion introduced by him is the belief in one God and the doctrines of morality.
>
> Brutus is supposed to have travelled into Egypt, and there to have learned the unity of the Deity, and the other purer doctrines, afterwards kept up in the mysteries.

Though there is none of it writ as yet, what I look upon as more than half the work is already done, for 'tis all exactly planned.

'It would take you up ten years?' [asked Spence.]

Oh, much less, I should think, as the matter is already quite digested and prepared.[1]

This bears the hallmark of Pope's most fervid neo-classicism, in attempting to do for English epic what Virgil did for the Latin. The Trojan Brutus makes a link between Pope's world and Virgil's, as Aeneas linked Virgil's with Homer's; and the best qualities of the English gentleman, benevolence, reason and mild Christianity, are shown in the plan prevailing over the superstitious priestcraft of Ancient Britain, as the more Roman mixture of piety and force prevailed in Latium. Pope had his moral and his hero, in short: he had everything except a passionate need to write an epic, to explain an otherwise unintelligible universe (such as fired Milton in his disappointment) – or, perhaps more vital yet, a feeling for the narrative drive by which epic is animated. The *Aeneid* is, beside the *Iliad* and *Odyssey*, an undramatic work; its driving power is political ('evidently a party piece' as Pope himself called it in a cooler moment);[2] but it is drama itself beside what the narrative of *Brutus* promised, the conversion of unreasonable people to reason in religion and politics. In addition, Pope's sense that English epic was indelibly Miltonic led him to the startling decision to attempt the work in blank verse – though he had always doubted whether 'a poem can support itself without [rhyme] in our language'.[3] The opening invocation, which is all that remains of the experiment, shows how self-consciously he negotiated the change, like a swan on dry land:

> The Patient Chief, who lab'ring long, arriv'd
> On Britains Shore and brought with fav'ring Gods
> Arts Arms and Honour to her Ancient Sons:
> Daughter of Memory! from elder Time
> Recall; and me with Britains Glory fir'd,
> Me, far from meaner Care or meaner Song,
> Snatch to thy Holy Hill of spotless Bay,
> My Countrys Poet, to record her Fame.[4]

The want of momentum in the verse as well as the subject may leave us concurring with Johnson:

> [Pope] laid aside his Epick Poem, perhaps without much loss to mankind; for his hero was Brutus the Trojan, who, according to a ridiculous fiction, established a colony in Britain. The subject therefore was of the fabulous age; the actors were a race upon whom imagination has been exhausted and attention wearied, and to whom the mind will not easily be recalled, when it is invited in blank verse, which Pope had adopted with great imprudence, and, I think, without due consideration of the nature of our language.[5]

For all the confidence and the planning, the epic was not written – the best comment on the undertaking of all. The inspiration for such a poem must come from somewhere deeper than a philosophy of reason and benevolence can touch; it is not to be assembled out of epic ingredients (heroes, morals, shipwrecks, and giants) like the *Receit to make an Epick Poem* he had written in his youth:

> Take out of any old Poem, History-books, Romance, or Legend, (for instance *Geffry of Monmouth* or *Don Belianis of Greece*) those Parts of Story which afford most Scope for long Descriptions: Put these Pieces together, and throw all the Adventures you fancy into one Tale. Then take a Hero, whom you may chuse for the Sound of his Name, and put him into the midst of these Adventures: There let him *work*, for twelve Books . . .[6]

The real materials for an epic were accumulating elsewhere – in Pope's disgust at the tone of public life under Walpole, in the metaphor of 'brass' we noted above, and, with mounting urgency in 1742, in another of those quarrels that made the life of a wit a warfare upon earth. This, with the uncompleted thoughts from the 1728 *Dunciad* on education that had been intended for the second book of the 'Opus Magnum', brought about a new version of the entire *Dunciad*.[7]

The enemy this time was someone who summed up in his smiling effrontery everything Pope felt about the cheerful corruption of the age as a whole: Colley Cibber, the poet laureate, on whose accession in 1730 the epigram had gone round,

> In merry old England it once was a rule,
> The King had his Poet, and also his Fool:
> But now we're so frugal, I'd have you to know it,
> That Cibber can serve both for Fool and for Poet.[8]

Cibber's appointment was not the first to debase the laureateship – his fuddled predecessor, Eusden, was rumoured to have accepted it for the 'Perquisite of Sack' alone – but it was a menacing honour to bestow on a man who, in his own sphere, was something of a Walpole. Cibber was a playwright and dictatorial actor–manager, with a grip as firm as the Lord Chamberlain's on the production of plays at Drury Lane theatre. He was famous for his mishandling of other playwrights, and he had already clashed with Pope and his friends in 1717, when he helped to bury a comedy in which Gay, Arbuthnot and Pope had collaborated. He made the celebrated decision to turn down the *Beggar's Opera* in 1728 (and was suspected of helping to get its sequel, *Polly*, banned, while mounting a plagiarised version of his own), but his most notorious achievement was in the character of author: as the creator of the runaway success of 1717, *The Non-Juror*, for which George I gave him £200 and his hand to kiss. This rabble-rousing play fed on anti-Catholic, anti-Jacobite tensions after the rising of 1715, and managed to link the opposition Tories, the Pretender, and any Catholic whatever to a Jesuit underground, in one excited shudder. The monarch's enthusiasm is easily explained by the tenor of the closing speech, which affirms, 'no Change of Government can give us a Blessing equal to our Liberty':

> *Grant us but this and then of Course you'll own*
> *To Guard that Freedom, GEORGE must fill the Throne.*[9]

Pope, a conspicuous non-juror himself (one who refused the oaths of allegiance to the new succession), deplored the 'great success of so damn'd a Play',[10] in the course of which his own works were repeatedly mentioned. But he recompensed himself by giving Cibber a line in the 1728 *Dunciad* (III, 320) and a place in *The Art of Sinking in Poetry*, among the 'Parrot' authors. Cibber allowed these provocations to pass for a while, apparently on the grounds that all publicity was good publicity, for nobody ever enjoyed exposure more. His mind was taken up with a project of his own – an autobiography, which opens with startling panache: 'But why make my follies publick? Why not?', and continues with mock-modesty and half-controlled silliness in a far-from-unfamiliar vein. In our day, Cibber would have been a chat-show host, famous for being famous, and just as carefully casual about his pretensions to seriousness. He freely admits to any potential critic,

> My Style is unequal, pert, and frothy, patch'd and party-colour'd, like the Coat of an *Harlequin*; . . . frequently aiming at Wit, without ever hitting the Mark; a mere Ragoust, toss'd up from the Offals of other Authors: My Subject below all Pens but my own, which, whenever I keep to, is flatly dawb'd by one eternal Egotism. . . . Nay, that this very Confession is no more a sign of my Modesty, than it is a Proof of my Judgment.[11]

In the course of these gyrations of mock-sincerity, however, he recapitulated the triumphs of his career as actor and stage-manager, and explained Pope's satirical fondness for his name as a cheap bait to catch the attention of the vulgar – almost a compliment to his fame. This helped bring the ancient quarrel (now twenty years old, and more) to a head, with each side expressing itself in an entirely characteristic way. Cibber struck as low as he could in a pamphlet of 1742, which was low even by the standards of the age, and Pope responded in 1743 by immortalising him in the last version of the *Dunciad*, where he displaces Theobald as the laureate of Dulness. We cannot tell exactly when the idea of the substitution came to Pope and he realised how his feelings of the last decade could be summarised by placing the brazen Cibber at the centre of his mock-epic (when he published an additional fourth book of the poem in 1742, the so-called *New Dunciad*, Cibber only occupied a fleeting line),[12] but it must have been immovably fixed by Cibber's above-mentioned pamphlet of a few months later, in which he conveniently 'remembered' having visited a brothel with Pope in his youth, and saved him from pox by hauling him off the whore he was about to enjoy. A large engraving of this act of friendship was supplied with the text, and instantly copied and offered for sale, sending the reverberations of delicious scandal round the town. Whatever feelings Pope experienced on the occasion, he compressed them into revising the original *Dunciad*[13] – and this epigram, 'On Cibber's Declaration that he will have the Last Word with Mr. Pope':

Quoth *Cibber* to *Pope*, tho' in Verse you foreclose,
I'll have the last Word, for by G——d I'll write Prose.
Poor *Colley*, thy Reas'ning is none of the strongest,
For know, the last Word is the Word that lasts longest.

THE *DUNCIAD* RENEWED, 1743

The word – and attendant image – that has lasted longest is that of
Cibber's impenetrable brass forehead. Was the old actor so hardened in effrontery? Very well, then, his metamorphosis should be
into all things hard and brazen, even as he acted the supreme hero
of his self-centred drama. 'What then remains?' Pope makes him
ask, superfluously, of the Goddess Dulness. And the answer
comes, in a wonderful parody of Medea:

> . . . Ourself. Still, still remain
> Cibberian forehead, and Cibberian brain. . . .

And, with mounting rapture,

> This brazen Brightness, to the 'Squire so dear;
> This polish'd Hardness, that reflects the Peer;
> This arch Absurd, that wit and fool delights. . . .
> (*Dunciad* B. I, 217–21)

And to underline the charge that Dulness is contagious, Pope
shows how Cibber's brazen gleam becomes the source of the
shining dullness of his aristocratic friends and fellow artists, by
delightful analogy with the way the stars collect their light from the
sun in *Paradise Lost* (VII, 364–6):

High on a gorgeous seat, that far out-shone
Henley's gilt tub, or Fleckno's Irish throne, . . .
Great Cibber sate: The proud Parnassian sneer,
The conscious simper, and the jealous leer,
Mix on his look: All eyes direct their rays
On him, and crowds turn Coxcombs as they gaze.
His Peers shine round him with reflected grace,
New edge their dulness, and new bronze their face.

So from the Sun's broad beam, in shallow urns,
Heav'ns twinkling Sparks draw light, and point their horns.
                                        (B. II, 1–2, 5–12)

Pope also dramatises what the hardness of the Cibberian forehead, and emptiness of the Cibberian brain, mean to the life at
court. It is not accidental that Cibber is laureate to George II, who
detested poetry; and Dulness anoints Cibber in excited anticipa-
tion of what sounds very much like the torpid reign of George
himself. Cibber is to follow where the fuddled Eusden led:

> Thou Cibber! thou, his Laurel shalt support,
> Folly, my son, has still a Friend at Court.
> Lift up your gates, ye Princes, see him come!
> Sound, sound ye Viols, be the Cat-call dumb!
> Bring, bring the madding Bay, the drunken Vine;
> The creeping, dirty, courtly Ivy join.
> And thou! his Aid de camp, lead on my sons,
> Light-arm'd with Points, Antitheses, and Puns.
> Let Bawdry, Bilingsgate, my daughters dear,
> Support his front, and Oaths bring up the rear:
> And under his, and under Archer's wing,
> Gaming and Grub-street skulk behind the King.
>   'O! when shall rise a Monarch all our own,
> And I, a Nursing mother, rock the throne,
> 'Twixt Prince and People close the Curtain draw,
> Shade him from Light, and cover him from Law;
> Fatten the Courtier, starve the learned band,
> And suckle Armies, and dry-nurse the land:
> 'Till Senates nod to Lullabies divine,
> And all be sleep, as at an Ode of thine.'
>   (B. I, 299–318)

At the court of Dulness, or George, the fine frenzy of poetical
inspiration collapses into drunkenness ('the drunken Vine') and
grovels to power ('the creeping, dirty, courtly Ivy join'). Poetry
becomes a matter of verbal frivolity ('Points, Antitheses, and
Puns'), or those last, low refuges of incoherent minds, 'Bawdry,
Bilingsgate . . . and Oaths'. The Laureate's annual Ode proves a
mere 'Lullaby' to the kind of Prince Dulness sighs for: tightly
curtained from his 'People', shaded from 'Light' and 'Law', in a

country where courtiers and armies 'fatten', but the learned 'starve'. She asks nothing more than to be his 'Nursing mother' and to 'rock the throne' like a cradle – ''Till Senates nod', and by implication, the rest of the country too. In this vision of Pope's, what is lost with the supremely responsible, self-conscious language that we call poetry is not just an artistic issue – it extends to political freedom as well. The craving for mental repose leads inevitably to irresponsibility, and the kind of monarch who will remove that burden from his subjects' shoulders: a monarch divided from his people, above the reach of law, supported by a standing army, and never contradicted by Parliament. George II is not merely Dulness's dream, but the product of the collective longings of a drowsy nation.[14]

Cibber and regal Dulness would labour in vain to smother the moral energies of the country if education were promoting thought, responsibility, and mental freedom. But in the new Book IV, educators are found crowding to the throne of Dulness to assure her that they do nothing of the kind, whether at the public schools, the universities, or on the Grand Tour. This is where Pope inserts his thoughts on education from the unfinished 'Opus Magnum', based on the long-held conviction that his own irregular education had been a blessing – permitting, as it had, the natural development of his curiosity and taste, unshackled by rote-learning, and unmenaced by the rod. Busby, the famous headmaster of Westminster School, who had tyrannised Dryden in his time, boasts complacently to Dulness of the narrow access he permits his boys to knowledge:

> Plac'd at the door of Learning, youth to guide,
> We never suffer it to stand too wide.
> To ask, to guess, to know, as they commence,
> As Fancy opens the quick springs of Sense,
> We ply the Memory, we load the brain,
> Bind rebel Wit, and double chain on chain,
> Confine the thought, to exercise the breath;
> And keep them in the pale of Words till death.
>
> (B. IV, 153–60)

This education severs the connection between imagination and perception ('as Fancy opens the quick springs of Sense'), and upsets the necessary balance between what the student takes in, and gives out. When the imagination has been rebuffed, and the memory overloaded, the result is a young bore very like the old bore who teaches him – someone for whom words are an end in themselves ('and keep them in the pale of Words till death').

What the public school has begun, the university happily continues. The central humanist discipline, the study of the classics, is presided over by scholars like Richard Bentley, who is really only Theobald in a more imposing guise. His discovery of a missing letter in the texts of Homer, the 'digamma', is a brilliant stroke of philology; but it licenses an egotism that elsewhere shrivels the study of the classics into debates on trivia: the pronunciation of 'C' in Latin (is it 'K'?); the explanation of obscure vocabulary via yet obscurer authors (to demonstrate the pedant's reading); the preference for fragments over complete texts – and the critical pertinacity that converts even complete texts into fragments; in short, an obsession with the 'hairs and pores' of the body of learning, as absurd as it is disgusting:

> 'Roman and Greek Grammarians! know your Better:
> Author of something yet more great than Letter;
> While tow'ring o'er your Alphabet, like Saul,
> Stands our Digamma, and o'er-tops them all.
> 'Tis true, on Words is still our whole debate,
> Disputes of *Me* or *Te*, of *aut* or *at*,
> To sound or sink in *cano*, O or A,
> Or give up Cicero to C or K.
> Let Freind affect to speak as Terence spoke,
> And Alsop never but like Horace joke:
> For me, what Virgil, Pliny may deny,
> Manilius or Solinus shall supply:
> For Attic Phrase in Plato let them seek,
> I poach in Suidas for unlicens'd Greek.
> In ancient Sense if any needs will deal,
> Be sure I give them Fragments, not a Meal;
> What Gellius or Stobæus hash'd before,
> Or chew'd by blind old Scholiasts o'er and o'er.
> The critic Eye, that microscope of Wit,
> Sees hairs and pores, examines bit by bit:
> How parts relate to parts, or they to whole,
> The body's harmony, the beaming soul,
> Are things which Kuster, Burman, Wasse shall see,

When Man's whole frame is obvious to a *Flea*.'
(B. IV, 215–38)

Whatever Bentley pretends, the largest question in classical studies is the supremacy of his own ego, and all other contenders for the place are 'hash'd' in advance. (Pope is remembering that Bentley produced a patronising edition of Horace, and one of *Paradise Lost* in which innumerable 'substandard' lines were bracketed; as Bentley introduces himself to Dulness, he is her '"mighty Scholiast, whose unweary'd pains/Made Horace dull, and humbled Milton's strains."' (211–12))

The effect on a young mind of Bentley's classical training is either to produce an inferior, but similarly conceited pedant, or a bewildered student determined never to touch his textbooks once he graduates. And all other schools of knowledge at the university take the same tone; as Bentley boasts,

'What tho' we let some better sort of fool
Thrid ev'ry science, run thro' ev'ry school?
Never by tumbler thro' the hoops was shown
Such skill in passing all, and touching none.'
(B. IV, 255–8)

The student released from the obligation of 'tumbling' very naturally turns his back on the entire circus. Information that was never internalised into knowledge, dead languages that never developed living significance, drop away as if they had never been:

'Thence bursting glorious, all at once let down,
Stunn'd with his giddy Larum half the town.
Intrepid then, o'er seas and lands he flew:
Europe he saw, and Europe saw him too.'
(B. IV, 291–4)

What impels him on the Grand Tour is not a passion for civilisation, but Life: foreign brothels, foreign courts, foreign fashion and foreign food. As the tutor of a young nobleman explains to Dulness, in presenting his charge:

'Led by my hand, he saunter'd Europe round,
And gather'd ev'ry Vice on Christian ground;

> Saw ev'ry Court, heard ev'ry King declare
> His royal Sense, of Op'ra's or the Fair;
> The Stews and Palace equally explor'd,
> Intrigu'd with glory, and with spirit whor'd;
> Try'd all *hors-d'œuvres*, all *liqueurs* defin'd,
> Judicious drank, and greatly-daring din'd;
> Dropt the dull lumber of the Latin store,
> Spoil'd his own language, and acquir'd no more;
> All Classic learning lost on Classic ground;
> And last turn'd *Air*, the Echo of a Sound!'
>
> (B. IV, 311–22)

The final product is the English milord, '"half-cur'd, and perfectly well-bred"' (l.323), ready to inherit the family estate and propagate the species via the foreign 'Venus' he brings home – a posterity that is guaranteed in advance to 'prop the Throne' of Dulness, and any other that might spring to mind:

> 'So may the sons of sons of sons of whores,
> Prop thine, O Empress! like each neighbour Throne,
> And make a long Posterity thy own.'
>   Pleas'd, she accepts the Hero, and the Dame,
> Wraps in her Veil, and frees from sense of Shame.
>
> (B. IV, 332–6)

Pope's final shafts are reserved for those who survive the education system with a genuine passion for some area of knowledge: not a large area, but one they can call their own. 'Virtuosos useless' is his dry summary of the theme in his original notes.[15] These men are the specialists in the emergent sciences, who do not seem absurd to us – but that is because we do not expect a specialist in plant-breeding or lepidoptera to have an overview of the relation of his science to wisdom at large. For Pope, such narrow mental concentration was the equivalent of physical deformity: it employed the brain in a way that weakened its proper functioning, converting scrupulosity into mania, and research into mere acquisitiveness. The virtuoso is an overgrown child in his view, making a toy of knowledge; but that, of course, is exactly what Dulness most approves of, and she receives the results of the virtuosos' efforts with the happy complacency of an infant teacher presiding over the Nature Table:

Then thick as Locusts black'ning all the ground,
A tribe, with weeds and shells fantastic crown'd,
Each with some wond'rous gift approach'd the Pow'r,
A Nest, a Toad, a Fungus, or a Flow'r.

(B. IV, 397–400)

In this realm of myopia and disproportionate passion, each special-
ism clashes painfully with the others. A carnation-grower pleads to
Dulness for justice, against the butterfly-collector who trampled
his prize bloom in the heedless chase. His prattling pathos is
Pope's whole argument embodied:

> The first thus open'd: 'Hear thy suppliant's call,
> Great Queen, and common Mother of us all!
> Fair from its humble bed I rear'd this Flow'r,
> Suckled, and chear'd, with air, and sun, and show'r,
> Soft on the paper ruff its leaves I spread,
> Bright with the gilded button tipt its head,
> Then thron'd in glass, and nam'd it CAROLINE:
> Each Maid cry'd, charming! and each Youth, divine!
> Did Nature's pencil ever blend such rays,
> Such vary'd light in one promiscuous blaze?
> Now prostrate! dead! behold that Caroline:
> No Maid cries, charming! and no Youth, divine!
> And lo the wretch! whose vile, whose insect lust
> Lay'd this gay daughter of the Spring in dust.
> Oh punish him, or to th'Elysian shades
> Dismiss my soul, where no Carnation fades.'

(B. IV, 403–18)

The impermeable lepidopterist shrugs off the guilt with a specialist's assurance:

> 'I saw, and started from its vernal bow'r
> The rising game, and chac'd from flow'r to flow'r.
> It fled, I follow'd; now in hope, now pain;
> It stopt, I stopt; it mov'd, I mov'd again.
> At last it fix'd, 'twas on what plant it pleas'd,
> And where it fix'd, the beauteous bird I seiz'd:
> Rose or Carnation was below my care;
> I meddle, Goddess! only in my sphere.

> I tell the naked fact without disguise,
> And, to excuse it, need but shew the prize;
> Whose spoils this paper offers to your eye,
> Fair ev'n in death! this peerless *Butterfly*.'
> (B. IV, 425–36)

Dulness finds it quite impossible to adjudicate between them: '"My sons! (she answer'd) both have done your parts:/Live happy both, and long promote our arts"' (437–8) – for both have pledged what gives her most security, to 'meddle only in their sphere'. It is the tendency of Reason to pass from the study of parts to wholes, and from wholes to causes, that most disturbs her:

> 'O! would the Sons of Men once think their Eyes
> And Reason giv'n them but to study *Flies*!
> See Nature in some partial narrow shape,
> And let the Author of the Whole escape:
> Learn but to trifle; or, who most observe,
> To wonder at their Maker, not to serve.'
> (B. IV, 453–8)

Lest we suppose these trivial occupations of the brain are as innocent in adults as they would be in children, Pope underlines the point to which they tend: a moral stupidity, where ethical questions are pursued no more connectedly than scientific ones. The luxurious torpor Dulness promotes is just what the human ego yearns for. She relieves her courtiers of the burden of conceiving anything greater than themselves, and releases them into a world of Nature which kindly operates at their own level – or a little above it:

> Yet by some object ev'ry brain is stirr'd;
> The dull may waken to a Humming-bird;
> The most recluse, discreetly open'd, find
> Congenial matter in the Cockle-kind;
> The mind, in Metaphysics at a loss,
> May wander in a wilderness of Moss . . .
> (B. IV, 445–50)

But in a short life, the proper study of mankind is not moss.[16]

The common factor in all this satire on the misuse of the brain is the miniaturisation implied – the sense that the human scale is dwindling to that of insects, whether it is the flea obsessed with the 'hairs and pores' of a classical text, the locust-swarm of virtuosos 'black'ning all the ground', or the silk-worm, whose slender thread of criticism 'clouds' a work 'all o'er' ('"For thee explain a thing till all men doubt it,/And write about it, Goddess, and about it"' (251–2)). The most menacing of all these similes is of bees swarming about their queen, by which Pope suggests that it is not, finally, a matter of education, but of instinctual dulness in all spheres of life and art. 'The sons of Dulness want no instructors in study, nor guides in life: they are their own masters in all Sciences, and their own Heralds and Introducers into all places,' as he sardonically observes (note to l.75):

> The young, the old, who feel her inward sway,
> One instinct seizes, and transports away.
> None need a guide, by sure Attraction led,
> And strong impulsive gravity of Head:
> None want a place, for all their Centre found,
> Hung to the Goddess, and coher'd around.
> Not closer, orb in orb, conglob'd are seen
> The buzzing Bees about their dusky Queen.
>   The gath'ring number, as it moves along,
> Involves a vast involuntary throng,
> Who gently drawn, and struggling less and less,
> Roll in her Vortex, and her pow'r confess.
>   (B. IV, 73–84)

Nothing could better convey the underlying allure of Dulness: freedom from the burden of individuation, utter security in nothingness, and the sense of buzzing power in the mass, which leaves the solitary individual vulnerable indeed (one bee-sting is an irritation, but a swarm of bees can kill).

The accuracy of Pope's metaphor is nicely shown by Cibber's response to being forewarned about the revised *Dunciad*: there is safety in numbers, he cries, as he rallies his support:

> Let us then, Gentlemen, who have the Misfortune, to lie thus at the Mercy of those whose natural Parts happen to be stronger than our own; let us, I say, make the most of our Sterility! let us double and treble the Ranks of our Thickness, that we may form

an impregnable Phalanx and stand every way in Front to the Enemy![17]

The jauntiness does not in the least disguise the menace; and the Goddess's own complacent sense that she has such numbers on her side explains the deep aggression that lurks in her pillowy nothingness. She is truly an imperial power, though her weapon is only an enormous yawn; yawns, however, are irresistibly catching, and hers passes rapidly from the Church to the State, to overwhelm Walpole (Palinurus), the army, the navy, and the nation:

> More had she spoke, but yawn'd – All Nature nods:
> What Mortal can resist the Yawn of Gods?
> Churches and Chapels instantly it reach'd;
> (St James's first, for leaden Gilbert preach'd)
> Then catch'd the Schools; the Hall scarce kept awake;
> The Convocation gap'd, but could not speak:
> Lost was the Nation's Sense, nor could be found,
> While the long solemn Unison went round:
> Wide, and more wide, it spread o'er all the realm;
> Ev'n Palinurus nodded at the Helm:
> The Vapour mild o'er each Committee crept;
> Unfinish'd Treaties in each Office slept;
> And Chiefless Armies doz'd out the Campaign;
> And Navies yawn'd for Orders on the Main.
>
> (B. IV, 605–18)

What in the 1728 *Dunciad* was a prophecy, in this version becomes an accomplished fact. It may seem a long step from a comprehensive yawn to the end of civilisation, but Pope knows that just as it was put together by human effort, so the failure of effort can undo it all again. As he menacingly observes,

> Do not thou, gentle reader, rest too secure in thy contempt of these Instruments. Remember what the Dutch stories somewhere relate, that a great part of their Provinces was once overflow'd, by a small opening made in one of their dykes by a single Water-Rat.
>
> (B. III, 333n.)

If the world emerged from chaos through the power of the word, so the 'uncreating word' of Dulness can return it to its first chaos. All that is required is for philosophy, religion, art, imagination, science, and sense, all the forms of connected significance that make up the structure of the civilised brain, to burn themselves out like so many fireworks in a final, cataclysmic display, and we are back where we began. The 'great Anarch', Dulness, remains alone in the dark formlessness that is her habitat, in a dreadful parody of Genesis ('And the earth was without form, and void; and darkness was upon the face of the deep', 1:2). Pope rewrites the concluding prophecy of the 1728 version with a compression of metaphor and vigour of rhetoric that, by common agreement, he never surpassed:

> She comes! she comes! the sable Throne behold
> Of *Night* Primæval, and of *Chaos* old!
> Before her, *Fancy's* gilded clouds decay,
> And all its varying Rain-bows die away.
> *Wit* shoots in vain its momentary fires,
> The meteor drops, and in a flash expires.
> As one by one, at dread Medea's strain,
> The sick'ning stars fade off th'ethereal plain;
> As Argus' eyes by Hermes' wand opprest,
> Clos'd one by one to everlasting rest;
> Thus at her felt approach, and secret might,
> *Art* after *Art* goes out, and all is Night.
> See skulking *Truth* to her old Cavern fled,
> Mountains of Casuistry heap'd o'er her head!
> *Philosophy*, that lean'd on Heav'n before,
> Shrinks to her second cause, and is no more.
> *Physic* of *Metaphysic* begs defence,
> And *Metaphysic* calls for aid on *Sense*!
> See *Mystery* to *Mathematics* fly!
> In vain! they gaze, turn giddy, rave, and die.
> *Religion* blushing veils her sacred fires,
> And unawares *Morality* expires.
> Nor *public* Flame, nor *private*, dares to shine;
> Nor *human* Spark is left, nor Glimpse *divine*!
> Lo! thy dread Empire, CHAOS! is restor'd;
> Light dies before thy uncreating word:
> Thy hand, great Anarch! lets the curtain fall;
> And Universal Darkness buries All.
>
> (B. IV, 627–56)[18]

Conclusion

DEATH OF POPE, 1744

During the revision of the *Dunciad* Pope recognised that his chronic bad health had taken a critical turn. He had required for some time a kind of iron case to support his collapsed spine and rib-cage (the final effect of his spinal tuberculosis), but now the combination of breathlessness and a kidney complaint rendered him very weak. He had planned to publish a complete annotated edition of all his works with the aid of his new friend Warburton, however, and expressed an anxious sense that his life would not be truly complete without it: 'I *must* make a perfect edition of my works, and then I shall have nothing to do but to die'.[1] The *Dunciad, Essay on Man,* and *Essay on Criticism* did appear in this edition (with notes made distressingly elephantine by his co-editor's scholarly humour) and the *Epistles to Several Persons* were printed just in time for Pope to send out advance copies. Spence recorded a sickroom conversation with him that demonstrates how even death, for an eighteenth-century artist, is a matter of form and allusion – underpinned by a sense of reality:

> Here am I, like Socrates, distributing my morality among my friends, just as I am dying. (On sending about some of his Ethic Epistles as presents, about three weeks before we lost him.)
>
> 'I really had that thought several times when I was last with you, and was apt now and then to look upon myself like Phaedo' [said Spence].
>
> That might be, but you must not expect me to say anything like Socrates at present.[2]

Pope declined through March and April 1744, attended by a variety of disputatious doctors and 'dying', as he pleasantly remarked, 'of a hundred good symptoms!' He rose from his sickbed to dine with the many guests who came to pay their last respects, and his closest friends remained in constant attendance throughout May, when he took to his bed for the last time and received the Catholic rites. As his friend David Mallet reported his death to Lord Orrery,

On Monday last I took my everlasting Farewell of him. He was enough himself to know me, to enquire after Mrs Mallet's Health, and anxiously to hasten his Servant in getting ready my Dinner, because I came late. The same social Kindness, the same friendly Concern for those he loved, even in the minutest Instances, that had distinguished his heart through Life, were uppermost in his Thoughts to the last.

He dyed on Wednesday [30 May 1744] about the Middle of the Night, without a Pang, or a Convulsion, unperceived of those that watched him, who imagined he was only in a sounder Sleep than ordinary. – But I cannot go on.[3]

His estate was not conspicuously large, having been diminished by many charities in his lifetime, but in addition to property he left £6000, which was laid out in various bequests to friends. The chief beneficiary was Martha Blount, to whom was bequeathed the use of the estate for life.

The quietness of Pope's end was doubtless not what the Dunces wished for him – but it seems a fitting conclusion to a literary life remarkable for steadiness of discipline, and the deliberate pursuit of a single goal. It is common for artists to aim in their lives for something beyond their powers, and regard their finished works as unsatisfying fragments of some greater whole. Pope was no exception, in his grandiose plan for 'reforming the mind'; but he does differ, in the way the fragments of that plan stand by themselves, having found their proper form in spite of authorial intention. He was unusual, that is, in having both the overreaching energy of genius, and the critical judgement necessary to keep it within useful bounds. He felt the inner imperative of the various forms he used, and allowed them to fulfil their natures as epistles, mock-epics, essays, and imitations, in a way that saved him from the common fate of poets – to have invested their best energies in their worst products, to have written much that would be read, and much that would not.

Perhaps, too, he had his wish in another sense: for the strength of the Romantic backlash against him is a tribute to how deeply his works did penetrate the eighteenth-century mind, leaving a younger generation no way to find its own voice save by wholesale repudiation. The conspicuous lull between Pope and Wordsworth is perhaps also traceable to a feeling that Pope's poetry left other poets with very little to do: he had put together, as Byron implied, a complete archive of culture, which the surviving world would gladly snatch from the wreck if England should ever sink beneath the waves. He had brought the Homeric past into the present, and uncovered the foundations of western literature (the *Iliad* and *Odyssey* translations), he had played the Homeric perspective over modern manners and choices (*The Rape of the Lock*), he had given women a new role and passions of their own (*To a Lady*, *Eloisa*), he had told man what he was and where his happiness lay (*Essay on Man*), he had made morality as interesting as satire (*Imitations of Horace*), and he had described how civilisation is put together or undone inside every human brain (*The Dunciad*). If this was not 'reforming' the mind, it was something better: raising its self-consciousness, and putting it more completely in its own keeping.

What made it all possible was his ability to balance powerfully opposed forces – most obviously, his punishing rationality, and his creative imagination. Considering how much of his intelligence is that of a literal-minded editor, we may be grateful that he managed to yoke it to creative purposes as consistently as he did, and that most of his footnotes and commentaries on his own work increase our pleasure (as in the notes to the *Iliad*) or contribute to the joke (as in *The Dunciad*). Warburton's ponderous edition of 1751 is a dark indication of what Pope's powers might have led to, if unleavened by creative tact. An equally unexpected conjunction is his anarchic sense of humour and powerful seriousness. When the two are brought together, as in the mock-epics, we enjoy the fine flexibility of a mind in which all belief is enlivened by doubt, and the sacred has learned to take a joke – to the great liberation of both author and reader.

A similar ability shows in the other notable balancing acts of Pope's life: as a genius, and as a cripple. He was keenly aware that 'one misfortune of extraordinary geniuses is that their very friends are more apt to admire than to love them.'[4] Pope did move his friends' love, as is palpable in Mallet's letter to Orrery, by making conspicuous show of his own affection and by abstaining from taking any of the usual liberties of genius. He accepted, even solicited, their criticism; and when he found himself well corrected by a stranger, could equally 'kiss the rod' and make a friend of his critic. The Joseph Spence whose anecdotes we have so often quoted began his acquaintance with Pope as the author of an *Essay on Pope's Odyssey*, which blamed as well as praised; and Pope candidly admitted where criticism was justified, when he pursued the author and earnestly invited him to Twickenham. His motive in behaving so properly in the face of criticism seems to have been underpinned by a sense of utility: where his work was concerned he would 'make use of ev'ry Friend – and ev'ry Foe'.

If we are looking for a single thread to unite his literary life, we may find it here, in his passion for usefulness. He wished his poetry to be useful to mankind; and everything that contributed to that end had his undivided attention. The controlling power of this passion may explain Pope's poise in that other balancing act of his life, his deformity. Even this had its usefulness, in concentrating his mind on the realm of the imagination, in which he was free, whole, and on equal terms with any man; and when the inadequacy of his organism threatened to upset that balance, he withstood cruel headaches, and the torturing of his internal organs, with a stoicism very like indifference. It is because he wished to be useful most of all that he eluded those two pitfalls of the crippled, aggressive self-pity and aggressive pride. He chose rather to live in a realm where there were no excuses – and either his verses were as good as he could make them, and useful to his civilisation, or they were not. As Johnson sums up the severity of his code,

He did not court the candour, but dared the judgment of his reader, and, expecting no indulgence from others, he shewed none to himself.[5]

APPENDIX

Pope's Versification

Probably no factor has contributed so much to the ups and downs of Pope's reputation as his versification. Considered as little short of miraculous in his own day, it became the butt of Romantic scorn: Keats thought the end-stopped heroic couplet puerile ('They sway'd about upon a rocking horse,/And thought it Pegasus') and viewed its construction as a matter of mere carpentry ('ye taught a school/Of dolts to smooth, inlay, and clip, and fit,/Till, like the certain wands of Jacob's wit,/Their verses tallied. Easy was the task:/A thousand handicraftsmen wore the mask/Of Poesy').

Respect for Pope's formidable skills has reasserted itself, particularly among specialists, but the first-time reader of Pope may well find himself back on Keats's rocking horse when he attempts to read the verse aloud. He may also be inclined to second the accusation of 'carpentry', when he sees from the footnotes of the Twickenham edition how many of Pope's lines are constructed out of parts of others. This appendix attempts to put these objections in perspective.

(a) MONOTONY

The 'rocking-horse' sensation of the heroic couplet begins in the eye of the modern reader, which is strongly drawn to the final rhyme. Pope's rhythms are actually subtle and carefully graded within the line according to the subject; as when he describes the torpid readers in the *Dunciad*, who:

> Thro' the long, heavy, painful page drawl on;
> Soft creeping, words on words, the sense compose,
> At ev'ry line they stretch, they yawn, they doze . . .

Contrast the lively management of the tickling test:

> While thus each hand promotes the pleasing pain,
> And quick sensations skip from vein to vein.

Nor does the sense necessarily end with the line: Pope will run across a line-ending if the effect is dramatic. He compares the nodding heads above to swaying pines:

> As to soft gales top-heavy pines bow low
> Their heads, and lift them as they cease to blow . . .

and the same enjambment gives impetus to a dive:

> Not so bold Arnall; with a weight of skull,
> Furious he dives, precipitately dull.

Even where the lines are all end-stopped, it is not a matter of confining the sense to twenty syllables. Pope writes in verse paragraphs, and the force of the couplets is cumulative, as in the acclamation of Cibber, a *tour-de-force* of rhetorical flexibility:

> She ceas'd. Then swells the Chapel-royal throat:
> 'God save king Cibber!' mounts in ev'ry note.
> Familiar White's, 'God save king Colley!' cries;
> 'God save king Colley!' Drury-lane replies:
> To Needham's quick the voice triumphal rode,
> But pious Needham dropt the name of God;
> Back to the Devil the last echoes roll,
> And 'Coll!' each Butcher roars at Hockley-hole.

Pope also exploits the sensual power of words to a degree Keats himself might have envied: consider the sensuality of

> How here he sipp'd, how there he plunder'd snug
> And suck'd all o'er, like an industrious Bug,

and,

> As when a dab-chick waddles thro' the copse
> On feet and wings, and flies, and wades, and hops . . .

The reader who attends to these subtleties will not complain of monotony, and will earn the gratitude of Pope, who was wont to complain that he had made his verses imitate the thing described 'much oftener than anyone minds it'. (The above examples are taken from the *Dunciad* alone: they could be multiplied almost indefinitely from the other works.)

(b) VERSE CARPENTRY

Keats's account of producing heroic couplets by 'inlaying, clipping and fitting' is not actually wide of the mark. Where he errs is in asserting 'easy was the task', for those who carpentered verses without sufficient attention to their meaning, as well as their form, were Pope's Dunces, the forgotten poets of the age. As anyone will attest who has ever tried to rhyme a couplet, it is very difficult to suppress the urge to say what one can, according to the rhymes available, rather than what one means. It takes a vast repertoire of rhymes and a flexible sense of line arrangement to permit a poet to express himself untrammelled. Pope set himself to acquire this repertoire from his earliest reading onwards (chiefly from his great mentor, Dryden); and since he confined his poetry almost entirely to the heroic couplet, the natural consequence was, as Johnson remarks, 'readiness and dexterity. By perpetual practice, language had, in his mind, a systematical arrangement; having always the same use for words, he had words so selected and combined as to be ready at his call'.

One example of this 'systematical arrangement' must suffice. It is unusually clear-cut, and the majority of Pope's arrangements are less traceable, but the indication it gives of the longevity and flexibility of couplet patterns is quite representative. This verse arrangement is associated with an atmosphere of doom, and has done considerable service before Pope takes it over:

> (In many a sweet rise, many as sweet a fall)
> A full-mouth *Diapason* swallowes all
> > (Crashaw, 1646)

> Till at the last your sap'd foundations fall,
> And Universal Ruine swallows all
> > (Dryden, 1673)

The fatal Day draws on, when I must fall;
And Universal Ruine cover all
       (Dryden, 1693)

Earth would not keep its place, the *Skies* would fall,
And universal Stiffness deaden All
       (Creech, 1697)

The *Veian* and the *Gabian* Tow'rs shall fall,
And one promiscuous Ruin cover all
       (Addison, 1705)

Pope uses it liberally for the various disasters of the *Iliad* and *Odyssey*:

'Till Darkness, or till Death shall cover all:
Let the War bleed, and let the Mighty fall!
       (*Iliad*)

When *Priam*'s Pow'rs and *Priam*'s self shall fall,
And one prodigious Ruin swallow All
       (ibid.)

Ilion shall perish whole, and bury All;
Her Babes, her Infants at the Breast, shall fall
       (ibid.)

Gods! shall one raging Hand thus level All?
What Numbers fell! what Numbers yet shall fall!
       (ibid.)

In blazing heaps the Grove's old Honours fall,
And one refulgent Ruin levells all
       (ibid.)

Here, far from *Argos*, let their Heroes fall,
And one great Day destroy, and bury all!
       (ibid.)

Whelm'd in thy Country's Ruins shalt thou fall,
And one devouring Vengeance swallow all
       (ibid.)

> Heav'd from the lowest Stone; and bury All,
> In one sad Sepulchre, one common Fall
> > (ibid.)

> The Sun shall see her conquer, till his Fall
> With sacred Darkness shades the Face of all
> > (ibid.)

> And make her conquer, till *Hyperion*'s Fall
> In awful Darkness hide the Face of all?
> > (ibid.)

> Now by the sword and now the jav'lin fall
> The rebel race, and death had swallow'd all
> > (*Odyssey*)

The reason why this couplet is well known is, of course, that it ends the climactic vision of the *Dunciad*:

> Thy hand, great Anarch! lets the curtain fall;
> And Universal Darkness buries All.

But its flexible application in Pope's repertoire is perhaps better exemplified by a less noticeable couplet satirising the theatre:

> A fire, a jig, a battle, and a ball,
> Till one wide Conflagration swallows all.

Nor is this the end of its useful existence: so long as this art of verse construction was understood, its rhyme and cadence continued to circulate – as in the poetry of Gray:

> Here mouldering fanes and battlements arise,
> > Turrets and arches nodding to their fall,
> Unpeopled monasteries delude our eyes,
> > And mimic desolation covers all.
> > > (1768)

I hope an example like this demonstrates that, if Pope's couplet is produced by 'clipping and fitting', it is not a matter of dull carpentry, but the subtlest marquetry, which can produce whatever picture is required.

Notes

Introduction

1. *Laureate of Peace: on the Genius of Alexander Pope* (London: Routledge, 1954), p.12.
2. James Reeves is the latest critic to insist on Pope's human clay, evidently tired of hearing Aristides called The Just; see *The Reputation and Writings of Alexander Pope* (London: Heinemann, 1976).
3. *Anton Chekhov: Five Plays*, trans. Ronald Hingley (Oxford: OUP, 1980), p.89.
4. Tom Mason, 'The Life of a Poet and the Life of a Man,' *Cambridge Quarterly*, 16, No.2 (1987), 153.
5. *The Twickenham Edition of the Poems of Alexander Pope*, ed. John Butt et al., 11 vols (London: Methuen, 1938–68), V, 16. Hereafter cited as *TE*.
6. Joseph Spence, *Observations, Anecdotes, and Characters of Books and Men*, ed. J.M. Osborn, 2 vols (Oxford: Clarendon, 1963), no. 407. Hereafter cited as Spence.
7. *TE*, IV, 159.
8. Samuel Johnson, 'Pope', *Lives of the Poets*, ed. G.B. Hill, 3 vols (Oxford: Clarendon, 1905), III, 200. Hereafter cited as Johnson.
9. For a full description of what he calls man's 'exosomatic evolution', see Karl R. Popper, *Objective Knowledge: An Evolutionary Approach* (Oxford: Clarendon, 1986), pp.235–46.
10. *Prose Works of Alexander Pope*, ed. Norman Ault and Rosemary Cowler, 2 vols (Oxford: Blackwell, 1936–86), I, 292. Hereafter cited as Pope, *Prose*.
11. *The Works of Lord Byron*, ed. Rowland E. Prothero, 13 vols (London: John Murray, 1901), V, 560.
12. *Boswell's Life of Johnson*, ed. G.B. Hill, rev. L.F. Powell, 6 vols (Oxford: Clarendon, 1950), V, 79.
13. *Memoirs of M. de Voltaire, Works*, ed. Arthur Friedman, 5 vols (Oxford: Clarendon, 1966), III, 253; quoted by Maynard Mack, *Alexander Pope: A Life* (New Haven and London: Yale University Press, 1985), p.447. Hereafter cited as Mack.

Chapter 1

1. Spence, no. 11.
2. Ibid., no. 23.
3. Ibid., no. 24.
4. *TE*, I, 59n.
5. Spence, no. 29.
6. Ibid., no. 22.
7. *Early Lives of Dante*, trans. Philip Wicksteed (London: King's Classics, 1904), p.12.

8. *Autobiographies* (London: Macmillan, 1966), pp.102–3.
9. Pope, *Prose*, I, 293.
10. Spence, nos 40, 38.
11. The earliest extant draft, from a letter of 1709. *The Correspondence of Alexander Pope*, ed. George Sherburn, 5 vols (Oxford: Clarendon, 1956), I, 68–9. Hereafter cited as *Correspondence*. The resemblance to Cowley is modified in the version Pope printed in 1717. A word may be timely on eighteenth-century printing conventions: names are italicised, and nouns capitalised (though the latter convention began to disappear in the 1720s).
12. For all these sources, see *TE*, VI, 5n.
13. *TE*, VI, 9n.
14. Written 1702, according to Pope, but published in this version 1712.
15. Spence, no. 194.
16. *Correspondence*, I, 211.
17. *TE*, I, 59n.
18. 'On *Pastorals*', in Pope, *Prose*, I, 103.
19. Jacob Tonson to Pope, 20 April 1706. *Correspondence*, I, 17.

Chapter 2

1. Pope, *Prose*, I, 295.
2. Spence, no. 13 (and note), 192.
3. Ibid., no. 135.
4. *Correspondence*, I, 235.
5. In a virulently personal review by John Dennis, 'Reflections Critical and Satyrical, upon a late Rhapsody, call'd, An Essay upon Criticism,' (1711); quoted by Mack, p.183.
6. *Correspondence*, I, 114.
7. Spence, no. 50 (note).
8. Johnson, III, 94.
9. Spence, no. 396 (see also no. 399).
10. The 'rape' of the lock is, strictly speaking, a Latinism for 'snatching away'.
11. Spence, no. 107.
12. In the dedicatory 'Letter' added to the poem in 1714, *TE*, II, 142. For a fuller account of the role of 'Machinery' in both epic and mock-epic, see my 'Of Gods and Men,' *Cambridge Quarterly*, 13, No.1 (1984), 1–20.
13. Johnson, III, 233–4.
14. *TE*, II, 143.
15. *TE*, II, 195.
16. *Correspondence*, I, 338.
17. Ibid.
18. Johnson, III, 235.
19. *The Poems of John Dryden*, ed. James Kinsley, 4 vols (Oxford: Clarendon, 1958), I, 180.
20. For a clearer explanation of this 'meeting' see my '"The Dear Ideas":

Pope on Passion', *Cambridge Quarterly*, 15, no. 3 (1986), 216–28.
21. The satire is, more precisely, of the psalm in Sternhold's versification, see Mack, p.298.
22. *TE*, II, 336.

Chapter 3

1. Spence, no. 192.
2. *The Iliad of Homer* (1712), in blank verse printed as prose, translated from the French of Anne Dacier (1711) by Broome, Oldisworth, and Ozell.
3. *Homer his Iliads* (1660), p.422.
4. For fuller details of this famous quarrel, and insight into the provocation Addison himself received, see Mack, pp.272ff.
5. See Johnson's similar account, III, 114.
6. For details of the dozen or so translations and the numerous secondary sources Pope regularly consulted, see the Introduction to *TE*, VII, sections II–III.
7. *Correspondence*, I, 219–20.
8. Spence, no. 30.
9. *On Translating Homer*, in *The Complete Prose Works of Matthew Arnold*, ed. R.H. Super, 11 vols (Ann Arbor: University of Michigan Press, 1960–77), I, 133–5.
10. Ibid., p.164.
11. *The Iliad of Homer*, trans. Richmond Lattimore (Chicago: University of Chicago Press, 1951), p.163. For the besetting vices of modern Homer translations, see H.A. Mason's *To Homer Through Pope* (London: Chatto, 1972), pp.179–206.
12. *Poems*, ed. Kinsley, III, 1055.
13. *Correspondence*, I, 44.
14. For details of this arrangement and the final effect, see the Introduction to *TE*, VII, section V (i).
15. The descent into the underworld in Broome's Book XI, for instance, is in Pope's best manner, and Broome acknowledged his 'daily revisal and correction' (*TE*, X, 378).
16. Mack, pp.412ff.
17. George Sherburn, *The Early Career of Alexander Pope* (Oxford: Clarendon, 1934), p.262.
18. *Correspondence*, II, 344.
19. See the deeply disingenuous footnotes to *Dunciad* A. III, 328 and B. I, 146.
20. See the discussion in Pope's interesting Postscript, *TE*, X, 387–91.
21. His sympathies lie with these 'amiable' and 'disinterested' characters; see his long footnotes on III, 53, and XVI, 512. For the effort he made to see Achilles from Homer's point of view, see my article, '"Aw'd by Reason": Pope on Achilles', *Cambridge Quarterly*, 9, no. 3 (1980), 197–202.
22. Fénelon's lucid adaptation of the story for purposes of moral

education at court (*Les Avantures de Télémaque*, 1699), gave the Odyssey an appealing 'modernity'.

23. The difference between the treatment of the gods in the two epics, and the poetical consequences, are considered in more detail in my above-mentioned article (Ch.2, n. 12).

24. He appealed in an essay 'Against BARBARITY to ANIMALS' (*Prose*, I, 107–14) and was the affectionate owner of a series of dogs called Bounce.

25. .See particularly Books XXIII–XXIV, and XXIII, 371n; XXIV, 291n.

Chapter 4

1. For a full description and an assessment of the relation between this aspect of Pope's work and his poetry see Mack, *The Garden and the City: Retirement and Politics in the Later Poetry of Pope* (Toronto and London: OUP, 1969).

2. 'I'll hire another's' – the house and land in which Pope invested so much money were only his on lease, from Thomas Vernon.

3. J.V. Guerinot, *Pamphlet Attacks on Alexander Pope, 1711–1744* (London: Methuen, 1969), pp.xlii–xliii.

4. *Correspondence*, I, 243.

5. Preface to *Works*, 1717, in *Prose*, I, 292.

6. See the elaborate annotations and emendations listed by Mack, *'Collected in Himself': Essays Critical, Biographical, and Bibliographical on Pope and Some of His Contemporaries* (Cranbury, NJ: Delaware University Press, 1982), pp. 179–93 and Appendix A.

7. 'On Pastorals', in Pope, *Prose*, I, 100.

8. *Shakespeare Restored*, pp.2–45.

9. *Correspondence*, II, 384.

10. Ibid., 387–8.

11. *TE*, V, 201n.

12. *Correspondence*, III, 57.

13. *The Persian Princess*, pp.1–2.

14. Ibid., p.61.

15. *Poems*, ed. Kinsley, I, 284.

16. The wider implications of Dulness are well conveyed by Aubrey Williams in *Pope's 'Dunciad': A Study of its Meaning* (London: Methuen, 1955), and Emrys Jones, 'Pope and Dulness', in *Pope: Recent Essays*, eds Maynard Mack and J.A. Winn (Brighton: Harvester, 1980), pp. 612–51.

17. The 'Advertisement' to the poem, *TE*, V, 8.

18. Williams, *Pope's 'Dunciad'*, p.64.

19. Ibid., p.75.

20. Mack, p.457.

21. Pope, *Prose*, II, 197.

22. 'A Letter to the Publisher' (signed Cleland, but in Pope's style), *TE*, V, 16.

23. Guerinot, *Pamphlet Attacks*, p.167. The engraving, which is much

superior both as satire and art, is reproduced by Mack, p.474.
24. *TE*, V, 133 (note to l.263).

Chapter 5

1. Johnson, III, 217.
2. *Essay on Man*, I, 16.
3. *TE*, V, 53.
4. Spence, no. 295.
5. Ibid., no. 302. The ambitious project is fully described in Miriam Leranbaum, *Alexander Pope's 'Opus Magnum' 1729–1744* (Oxford: Clarendon, 1977).
6. See below, pp.138–40.
7. As Ted Hughes has phrased it, 'Works go dead, fishing has to be abandoned, the shoal has moved on. While we struggle with a fragmentary Orestes some complete Bacchae moves past too deep down to hear. We get news of it later . . . too late.' (*London Magazine*, January 1971).
8. *Correspondence*, III, 213–14.
9. Ibid., III, 117.
10. Johnson, III, 243.
11. Richard Blackmore, *The Creation, a Philosophical Poem in Seven Books* (1712), I, 68–71.
12. 'To the Reader', *TE*, III, i, 6.
13. See the transcript in *TE*, III, ii, xx–xxii.
14. Spence, no. 300.
15. Hence their usual order of printing, which is not that of composition or publication – see *TE*, III, ii, xix–xx.
16. *Correspondence*, I, 432.
17. For Pope's paradoxical feelings about female frailty, and the connection between this poem and the *Rape of the Lock*, see my '"Dipt in the Rainbow": Pope on Women' in *The Enduring Legacy*, eds G.S. Rousseau and Pat Rogers (Cambridge: CUP, 1988), pp.51–62.
18. Shakespeare, Sonnet xviii.

Chapter 6

1. *TE*, V, 43.
2. *Correspondence*, III, 352.
3. The 'Advertisement' to the *Imitation of Hor. Sat. II, i*, *TE*, IV, 3.
4. *Henry James Letters*, ed. Leon Edel, 4 vols (Cambridge, Mass.: Harvard University Press, 1984), IV, 770.
5. The volumes of Pope's poetry and letters edited by Reverend Elwin (1871–2, completed by Courthope, 1881–9) roused Mark Pattison to remark, 'We are made to feel from beginning to end that the object had in view in editing Pope was to induce us to desist from reading him. Pope is a liar, a cheat, and a scoundrel, and his so-called poetry

is ungrammatical, ill-rhymed, unmeaning trash.' Sherburn, *Early Career*, p.22.

6. *TE*, IV, 3.
7. Spence, no. 321a.
8. Lady Mary Wortley Montagu, *Verses Address'd to the Imitator of the First Satire of the Second Book of Horace* (1733), see *Pope: The Critical Heritage*, ed. John Barnard (London: Routledge, 1973), pp.271–2.
9. Lady Mary's family preserved a tradition that the break followed on her receiving Pope's declaration of love with an immoderate fit of laughter; Pope's version was that their relationship ended when she pressed him to join her in writing a satire and he refused (see *TE*, IV, xv–xvii). Whatever the details, it is clear that their characters composed a volatile mix of strengths and weaknesses that could not harmonise for long. When wounded, each became more intensely aristocratic: Pope, the aristocratic-artist, Lady Mary the aristocratic *pur sang* (she observed unpleasantly that Pope and Swift were 'entitl'd by their Birth and hereditary Fortune to be only a couple of Link Boys', *Correspondence*, ed. Robert Halsband (Oxford: Clarendon, 1967), III, 57).
10. *Prose*, II, 444.
11. These fragments are listed in the Introduction, *TE*, IV, xxiii–xxiv.
12. See his sketch of the 'assiduity and slavery' of Lord Lifford and his sister, who were

> constantly – every night in the country, and three nights in the week in town – alone with the King and Queen for an hour or two before they went to bed, during which time the King walked about and talked to the brother of armies, or to the sister of genealogies, whilst the Queen knotted and yawned, till from yawning she came to nodding, and from nodding to snoring.
> *Memoirs*, ed. Croker (1848), I, 292.

13. Five mornings of the week he would spend walking with Queen Caroline at Hampton Court (his account is in the third person):

> These excursions put it also in his power to say things as from other people's mouths, which he did not dare to venture from his own, and often to deliver that as the effect of his observation which in reality flowed only from his opinion.
> Ibid., I, 262.

14. *The Works of Alexander Pope*, eds Whitwell Elwin and J.W. Courthope (1871–89), I, xxvi–xxvii.
15. 'Preface' to the 1737 Correspondence, *Prose*, II, 372.
16. Spence notes in 1735 that Pope has been discussing 'the modesty or prudery of not publishing one's own letters' (no. 349) – presumably implying that it is false modesty in an author. He would have been glad to know that Erasmus overcame his prudery with the same determination, deploring the similarly 'unauthorised' publication of his correspondence in his lifetime; see the sensible account of their predicament by J.A. Winn, *A Window in the Bosom: The Letters of*

Alexander Pope (New Haven: Archon, 1977), p.42.

17. If we except the simplistic Romantic definitions of 'sincerity' and 'falsity', De Quincey's description of Pope's mentality is quite accurate:

> There is nothing Pope would not have sacrificed, not the most solemn of his opinions, nor the most pathetic memorial from his personal experiences, in return for a sufficient consideration, which consideration meant always with *him* poetic effect. . . . He was evermore false, not as loving or preferring falsehood, but as one who could not in his heart perceive much real difference between what people affected to call falsehood, and what they affected to call truth.

   De Quincey's Works, 16 vols (Edinburgh: Black, 1862), XII, 34–5.
18. Anonymous pamphlet of 1742, *The Critical Heritage*, p.261.
19. Pope, *Prose*, II, 370.
20. *Correspondence*, I, 160.
21. *The Yale Edition of Horace Walpole's Correspondence*, ed. W.S. Lewis, in 48 vols (New Haven: Yale University Press, 1955), XXVIII, 292.
22. Johnson, III, 209.
23. *Correspondence*, I, 371–5; 147–8.
24. Johnson, III, 207.
25. Quoted by Mack, p.664. Gray was another admirer of the 'humanity' and 'goodness of heart, aye, and greatness of mind' evinced by the correspondence (Letter to Walpole, 3 February 1746).
26. Pope considered contemporary monarchs 'mere tradesmen', and he famously remarked, when the Prince of Wales taxed him with this dislike, that he loved 'princes better than kings, as one likes a young lion, before his fangs and claws are grown, better than an old one' (Spence, nos 591, 593).
27. Johnson, III, 247.

Chapter 7

1. Spence, no. 343.
2. Ibid., no. 545.
3. Ibid., no. 395.
4. *TE*, VI, 404.
5. Johnson, III, 189.
6. *The Guardian*, 10 June 1713, in *Prose*, I, 117.
7. The original sketch of what became Book IV (?1728) is printed by Mack (*'Collected in Himself'*, op. cit., pp.340–43). Pope was not at liberty to make any changes till the copyright reverted to him in the early 1740s.
8. Quoted by Pope in the 1735 edition of the *Dunciad*, *TE*, V, 187n. Cibber attributed it to Pope himself.
9. *The Non-Juror* (1718), p.76.
10. *Correspondence*, I, 347.

11. *An Apology for the Life of Mr Colley Cibber, Comedian* (1740), pp. 26–7.
12. 'Soft on her lap her Laureat son reclines', 1.20. This may have been the provocation to which Cibber responded with his pamphlet, or there may have been advance warning of Pope's intentions. There is some mystery surrounding a leaf of the revised *Dunciad* which 'a friend' sent to Cibber; see Spence, nos 253, 331, and *TE*, V, xxxiii–xxxv.
13. Much ink has been spilt on Pope's presumed mortification and on the likely truth of the anecdote. Pope's only comment is his drily credible remark to Spence, 'There was a woman there, but I had nothing to do with her of the kind that Cibber mentions, to the best of my memory – and I had so few things of that kind ever on my hands that I could scarce have forgot it, especially so circumstanced as he pretends' (no. 251). Cibber's patience in waiting 27 years to make use of this anecdote must raise some doubts.
14. For a contemporary application, see my 'Dulness and General Jaruzelski', in *Cambridge Quarterly*, 16, No.2 (1987), 95–109.
15. Mack, *'Collected in Himself'*, op. cit., p.341.
16. There is confirmation of Pope's mistrust of these pursuits in Spence's anecdote of Sir Isaac Newton, who, 'though he scarce ever spoke ill of any man, could scarce avoid it towards your virtuoso collectors and antiquarians. Speaking of Lord Pembroke once [noted antiquarian and President of the Royal Society], he said, 'Let him but have a stone doll, and he is satisfied. I can't imagine those gentlemen but as enemies to classical studies; all their pursuits are below nature.' (no. 876)
17. *The Egotist: Or, Colley upon Cibber* (1743), p.77 (anonymous pamphlet attributed to Cibber).
18. For the long gestation of this last couplet and some explanation of Pope's couplet art as a whole, see Appendix.

Conclusion

1. Spence, no. 622.
2. Ibid., no. 631.
3. Quoted by Mack, p.812.
4. Spence, no. 564.
5. Johnson, III, 221.

Further Reading

The liveliest and most authoritative writing about Pope dates from the eighteenth century. Joseph Spence collected anecdotes from Pope and his circle which have been admirably edited by James M. Osborn (Joseph Spence, *Observations, Anecdotes, and Characters of Books and Men*, 2 vols, Oxford: Clarendon, 1966). This is the shortest way to become acquainted with Pope's tone of voice and way of thinking. Johnson's *Life of Pope* (1781) is still the best biography, though it has been corrected in many particulars by later research. Johnson knew people who had known Pope and he understood his literary world from the inside, as well as sharing most of his values. It is a trenchant, long-considered account, which praises and condemns Pope in tones we can imagine him attending to. G. Birkbeck Hill's edition is standard, with engrossing footnotes (Samuel Johnson, 'Pope', *Lives of the Poets*, ed. G.B. Hill, 3 vols, Oxford: Clarendon, 1905, Volume III). Pope's correspondence is a genuine autobiography of at least part of his complex nature: it is edited with some of the correspondence of his circle by George Sherburn (*The Correspondence of Alexander Pope*, 5 vols, Oxford: Clarendon, 1956). The reader can puzzle over the violent responses of Pope's first critics, and the controversies aroused by each work, in *Pope: The Critical Heritage*, edited by John Barnard (Routledge: London and Boston, 1973) and over the hundreds of scurrilous pamphlets Pope withstood in J.V. Guerinot, *Pamphlet Attacks on Alexander Pope 1711–1744* (London: Methuen, 1969), an edition with excerpts and well-tempered commentary. Pope's essays and pamphlets have recently been edited in full (*Prose Works of Alexander Pope*, Vol. 1, ed. Norman Ault, Oxford: Blackwell, 1936; Vol. 2, ed. Rosemary Cowler, Oxford: Blackwell, 1986). Also available is *Selected Prose of Alexander Pope*, ed. Paul Hammond (Cambridge, CUP, 1987).

In the nineteenth century, Pope's name became a form of shorthand for whatever the Romantics, and later, the Victorians, were reacting against in the previous century. When he was praised, it was for his 'filigree' charm, and when he was damned it was for superficiality, the formality of his conventions, and his outworn poetic diction. He found a magnificent defender in Byron, however ('the moral poet of all civilisation'), and the exchanges between Byron and the prudish Rev. Bowles still make exhilarating reading (*The Works of Lord Byron*, ed. Rowland E. Prothero, 13 vols, London: Murray, 1901, Vol. V). The hostile Elwin–Courthope edition of Pope (1871–89) stands only as a monument to how *not* to read him.

The dust of these controversies was finally laid in our century by the editors of the standard 'Twickenham' Pope (*The Twickenham Edition of the Poems of Alexander Pope*, ed. John Butt et al., 11 vols, London: Methuen, 1938–68). Each volume has a full introduction and exhaustive annotation (the introduction to Vol. II, *The Rape of the Lock*, is particularly helpful). This indispensable work has been condensed into one volume, with selected annotations, for the general reader (*The Poems of Alexander Pope*, ed. John Butt, London: Methuen, 1963). Pope has had to wait considerably longer for a modern biography. The work was begun by George Sherburn's *Early Career of Alexander Pope* (Oxford: Clarendon, 1934) and completed recently by Maynard Mack's tender and comprehensive account of modern findings, *Alexander Pope: A Life* (New Haven and London: Yale University Press, 1985).

The following general studies may be found helpful: Reuben A. Brower, *Alexander Pope: the Poetry of Allusion* (Oxford: Clarendon, 1959); G. Wilson Knight, *Laureate of Peace: On the Genius of Alexander Pope* (London: Routledge, 1954) – reissued as *The Poetry of Pope, Laureate of Peace* (London: Routledge, 1965, a yeasty work of criticism, with its origins in Byron's defence of Pope); Patricia Meyer Spacks, *An Argument of Images: The Poetry of Alexander Pope* (Cambridge, Mass.: Harvard University Press, 1971); Geoffrey Tillotson, *On the Poetry of Pope* (Oxford: Clarendon, 1938, revised 1950) and *Pope and Human Nature* (Oxford: Clarendon, 1958); and Austin Warren, *Alexander Pope as Critic and Humanist* (Princeton: Princeton University Press, 1929). On particular aspects of Pope's poetry the following can be warmly recommended: Maynard Mack, *The Garden and the City: Retirement and Politics in the Later Poetry of Pope, 1731–43* (Toronto and London: OUP, 1969); H.A. Mason, *To Homer Through Pope: An Introduction to Homer's Iliad and Pope's Translation* (London: Chatto, 1972); Frank Stack, *Pope and Horace: Studies in Imitation* (Cambridge: CUP, 1985); Aubrey L. Williams, *Pope's 'Dunciad': A Study of its Meaning* (London: Methuen, 1955); J.A. Winn, *A Window in the Bosom: The Letters of Alexander Pope* (New Haven: Archon, 1977); and W.K. Wimsatt, *The Portraits of Alexander Pope* (New Haven and London: Yale University Press, 1965). The reader interested in Pope's Homer but intimidated by the size of the undertaking may find a condensed version helpful, prepared by the present author: *Pope's Iliad: A Selection with Commentary*, ed. F. Rosslyn (Bristol: Bristol Classical Press, 1985). R. Straus, *The Unspeakable Curll* (London: Chapman, 1927), gives an engaging insight into Grub Street.

Index